# Contents

# OPEN THE WINDOW

## Practical Ideas for the Lonely and Depressed

Joan Gibson

## Gateway Books, Bath
### & Interbook Inc, San Leandro, Calif.

10106

First published in 1985
by GATEWAY BOOKS
19 Circus Place,
Bath, BA1 2PV

Second printing 1986

in the U.S.A.: INTERBOOK Inc,
14895 E. 14th Street,
San Leandro, CA 94577

cover artist: Chrissie Snelling
cover design: Studio B, Bristol

Set in 11 point Sabon by
Mathematical Composition Setters Ltd,
of Salisbury,
Printed by WBC Print of Bristol
and bound by Ware of Clevedon

British Library Cataloguing in Publication Data:

Gibson, Joan
  Open the window : practical ideas for the lonely
  and depressed.
  1. Depression, Mental—Treatment   2. Self-care, Health
  I. Title
  616.85' 2706     RC537

ISBN 0-946551-17-0

# Foreword

## Loneliness is always part of life.

We may share the love of our family, the companionship of our friends, the challenges of our colleagues, but within ourselves we are always alone.

We can enjoy this aloneness, valuing our privacy, our ability to make our own decisions and to control our own life or we can fear loneliness, feeling the ache and chill of not being held and loved, feeling that our existence does not connect with anyone or anything.

Joan Gibson described this most terrible state when she wrote,

> I vividly remember being lost at about the age of four and feeling quite alone in an alien and hostile world. That feeling returned during my depression. I seemed to be completely isolated in the vastness of the universe.

Because loneliness is part of life we have to learn the skills of dealing with it. Some of us learn these skills naturally when we are children, but some of us do not. Or we may have learnt the skills but have forgotten them when some event wrenches us from the group we love and leaves us on our own.

In this book Joan Gibson reminds us through stories, poems and her own personal experiences, of the wisdom the human race has accumulated over the centuries about how to live alone.

This is a delightful book full of warmth, gentle humour and practical commonsense. Anyone who is lonely or who fears loneliness will find sustenance here. Joan Gibson quotes Paul Tillich,

> Our language has wisely sensed the two sides of man's being alone. It has created the word *loneliness* to express the pain of being alone and it has created the word *solitude* to express the glory of being alone.

She reminds us how to discover the joy and glory of solitude.

*Dorothy Rowe*

# Introduction

I'm not a curtain-peeper,
I'm lonely and I'm old.
It's not just curiosity,
I wouldn't be so bold!
I like to watch folk passing by
And see the children play,
And give a chuckle or a sigh,
"I used to be that way."

So if you see my curtain move,
Don't think, "Look, fancy that!"
But pop in for a cup of tea
Or maybe just a chat.
A little understanding
Or a gesture that's well meant,
You'll find me undemanding,
But I'll find you heaven-sent.

Some years ago, these pathetic lines were sent to a
women's magazine. I often wonder, as I walk along a
street past rows of blank or curtained windows, just how
many sad and lonely folk are sitting there in their rooms,
longing for companionship and yet, for one reason or
another, unable to find it. Loneliness is becoming a disease
of our time, and as one elderly widow said to me recently,
"It's a killer!". We need to discover how to deal with it, for
it is a condition with which we may all have to contend at

some point in our lives. By learning to understand it, and how best to cope with it, I believe that we can do much to lessen its terrors. Indeed, loneliness need not be a frightening prospect at all. The Jolly Miller of Dee lived alone and was more than content with his lot, declaring in the words of the old song, "I would not change my station for any other in life". More people live alone now, either from choice or necessity, than ever in the past, and many would like to know the secret of the miller's self-sufficiency.

Few of us would seek continuous solitude; it comes more naturally to human beings to live together in tribes, groups, pairs or families. We learn the companionship and the give and take of family life from earliest childhood, and no child, however deprived, is able to live an entirely solitary existence. If it becomes necessary to live alone later in life, new ways and new values must be learnt before this can be a pleasurable experience. We are accustomed to thinking that being alone is a great hardship. The criminal dreads solitary confinement far more than being in an overcrowded cell. To be marooned on a desert island is regarded as a terrible fate. However, being alone does not necessarily mean being lonely.

Human minds need to be stimulated by others' thoughts and actions, but equally need time to develop on their own. Perhaps we are the poorer because of the pressure of modern living, with its continual bombardment of sound from radio, transistor and television and the constant presence of other people, which leaves us with no time for thoughts of our own. There are many benefits and advantages in living alone, as this book sets out to show, but first we have to find out how to adapt ourselves to such a way of life. Regrettably, for many people who live alone, and particularly for the elderly, loneliness is a dreadful affliction. Once it has become established it is very hard to cure. It is important to realise that loneliness is a state of mind, and can therefore be overcome. It may, indeed, be necessary to live alone, but whether or not we are lonely is largely a matter of our own choice.

The human mind is amazingly adaptable. We have our five senses of taste, smell, touch, hearing and sight. If one of these is destroyed we find that the others can be developed to compensate. A blind person uses his hearing, for example, far more than those of us who can see. Of course, it is not easy for someone who loses his sight to learn to adapt. He has first to accept his blindness and not waste time in bitter and futile regrets for the past and the things he is now unable to do. He has to learn instead a whole new quality of life in which sound is all-important, and he will learn to do everyday things, like making a cup of tea, in a new way, by using touch and hearing instead of sight. People who learn to do this can be just as happy as those who can see. It is easier to understand how this is possible by trying to imagine that we all have an extra sense, telepathy for example, so that we can project our thoughts to others by a sort of inbuilt telephone system. If everyone could do this and then, suddenly, one person lost the power, it would still be possible for that person to enjoy a happy life. He would feel deprived at first, but he would soon adjust. We know this because we can live perfectly contentedly without the extra sense.

Therefore, in order to make a success of living alone, we have to adapt ourselves to a new pattern so that instead of loneliness and frustration we find fulfilment and satisfaction. Helen Keller, who from early childhood was blind, deaf and dumb, learnt to adapt herself and was able to live a happy and useful life. I have always remembered how she once said, "Never, never, never feel sorry for yourself."

Let us make this the starting point, and resolve not to look back, not to regret the past, not to waste time in trying to alter things that cannot be changed, but rather to consider how we can set about learning the technique of living alone contentedly and happily. I believe that the best way to achieve this is to develop a positive attitude to life. I have divided this book into three sections, and at the end of each have listed positive actions which may be taken, and negative ones which should be avoided if possible. Thus, instead of being defeated by loneliness, we may learn to fight and overcome it, so that it no longer poses a threat to our lives.

# Part I
# Stages of Loneliness

# 1 The Loneliness of Youth

Loneliness is an affliction not just of the elderly. There are solitary and withdrawn children in every school. During morning break time the playground will resound with cries of boisterous groups, laughing, chasing, quarrelling and generally enjoying themselves, but there will almost certainly be one child standing aloof from his or her fellows, watching passively and unable to join in.

There are many reasons why this should be so, and sometimes it is difficult to discover the cause. An only child, who has been brought up solely in the company of adults, may find it hard to react naturally to others of his own age. Children with a physical or mental handicap may also have special problems, as will those from broken homes, but sometimes a child just seems to be unusually shy or timid by nature. Parents will obviously be worried by this and wonder how best they can help.

Certainly much can be done, but great care is needed and friendships cannot be forced. Parents do not always realise how much a child can be harmed during his early formative years if he has not been encouraged to make contacts with others, both inside the family and without. It is not until he starts school that this becomes apparent.

When I was teaching, I remember a small girl being brought to the infants' reception class on her first day at school. She was a gamekeeper's child, having been brought up in an isolated lodge on a large estate. She had scarcely ever seen another child, her mother had kept her quietly at home, and being a rather morose person herself, had spent little time playing with or talking to her daughter. The experience of being plunged into a noisy and lively crowd of five-year-olds was so traumatic, that the little girl was terrified. For several days she refused to leave the safety of her desk, and it was weeks before she could be persuaded even to play with toys or join in any activity with her classmates.

Children should always be given opportunities of meeting and playing with others of their own age before starting school. When a child has brothers and sisters bringing their friends home, or can make contact with neighbours' children, this is no problem. In towns there are play groups and nursery schools in most areas, where children can learn to play happily together and become used to each other's company. However, if a child is very timid and afraid to leave his mother, it will not be helpful to force him into such large gatherings. In cases like this, it is better to take him to a park or playground where he will see and be with other children, but not necessarily become too involved with their play until he is ready to join in.

The mother of an only child can do a great deal to prepare him for school by inviting a neighbour's child round for an hour or so, and also by teaching her son how to share his playthings without resentment, how to give and take, to await his turn, to be willing to follow as well as to lead, and so on. Simple board games like 'Ludo' or 'Snakes and Ladders' help children to understand that we must sometimes accept setbacks and defeats, and learn to lose without bad temper or sulking. Parents need to give time to teach these values to their children, and in so doing will help to ensure that they will make friends happily and easily when they enter the competitive world of school.

But if they discover that a child is finding it difficult to make friends naturally, what should they do? It is not advisable to try to force friendships artificially, nor should parents interfere in children's quarrels, except of course to prevent undue violence. To complain to others parents that your child has been victimised will only serve to antagonise them and make it most unlikely that the quarrel will blow over. Children's feuds are usually very short-lived. "She's my best friend, and I hate her!" is a frequent remark of childhood.

On the other hand, it is often possible to encourage friendships. If your child has a particular interest, it will sometimes help to suggest he brings home a classmate with the same hobby so that they can compare notes. Friendship, at whatever age, grows best from shared pursuits – it cannot be bought or won with bribes.

The timid or withdrawn child needs to be given reassurance and encouragement. He wants to feel that he is good at doing *something*, so that even if he is hopeless at sport, slow at arithmetic, a duffer at reading and unable to sing in tune, he can, nevertheless, surpass all his fellow-pupils in his knowledge of birds, his ability to fly a kite, his skill in manipulating puppets, or whatever the case may be. A discerning parent will discover the child's particular interest and encourage him to develop it. There are many organisations for young children, such as Brownies and Cub Scouts, Sunday School or other church groups, dancing or gymnastic classes and, when they are older, sports and swimming clubs, which offer means of acquiring new skills in the company of others their own age. Keeping a pet and learning to care for it will often help a child to become more out-going, and a lively and friendly dog, or an appealing kitten, may sometimes be the means of introducing him into the company of others.

Sometimes, though, we worry overmuch when a child seems to have few friends. He should be encouraged and given every opportunity to mix with others, but should never be forced or made to feel that he is behaving unnaturally. A child can quickly sense parental concern and come to believe that he has failed to live up to what is expected of him. This can cause him to develop a sense of inferiority, to lose confidence in himself, and consequently become even more withdrawn.

Loneliness in adolescents can be an extremely painful experience. Most teenagers have the urge to conform and to be like their fellows, so that if they are unable to fit into the accepted pattern they feel outcasts and failures. They can suffer agonies of embarrassment, especially when they are with groups of other young people and find themselves left out of whatever activity is going on. It is better, in these circumstances, for them to avoid discos and other social events where they know they will be conspicuous and awkward, and try instead to join smaller groups where they will feel welcomed and needed, not pushed aside and ignored. Helping with a charity, in a hospital, an old people's home, a Sunday school, or even joining an evening class will bring opportunities of meeting and making friends with people in all age groups. One friendship will often pave the way to others.

Negative behaviour as a result of loneliness is certainly a hazard. Some youngsters will follow a gang, admiring the bravado of its leaders and hoping to share in their reflected glory. If rejected, they may turn to drink, drugs or glue sniffing to try to achieve by these means the happiness and satisfaction which life has so far denied them.

We are at our most vulnerable during the years of adolescence, and loneliness, with its associated feelings of failure and unworthiness, can be very hard to bear. Fortunately, it is also during these youthful years that we feel most strongly urged to support causes and ideals and to work on behalf of them. This is the best and positive action that a young person finding himself lost and lonely should take. By using his time and energy in helping to bring about something which he believes to be worthwhile, he is given an aim in life, forgets his sense of awkwardness, and because he will be in the company of others who share his interest, is most likely to find friends along the way.

# 2   The Loneliness of Middle Age

While we can be plunged into loneliness at any time in our lives, the middle years hold their own particular hazards. The children grow up and leave home, a move is made to another area, problems may develop in a marriage, and divorce, separation or bereavement can leave one partner to cope with life alone.

## Bereavement

Each of us, at some time or other in our lives, must go through this most harrowing experience of all, but for some the loss is almost unbearable, and the change in their pattern of normal living very hard to adjust to. Nothing can ever be as it was before for them. Those who are unmarried will face the loss of parents, other near relations and friends; but people who have been happily married over many years, who have been contented with each other's company, and who, when the children have left home, have drawn even closer to one another, are the most vulnerable when this partnership is broken by death. The great gap torn in their lives will seem unbridgeable, and they will feel completely lost and out of their depth in a world which appears to be largely uncaring and wrapped up in its own affairs.

One of the more hurtful things immediately following a death is the way in which the bereaved person so often finds himself avoided and shunned by many of his friends and neighbours. They may be embarrassed and feel that they do not know what to say; they fear upsetting the widow or widower and so they avoid making contact. Yet this is usually the very time when, even if it brings tears, it is a relief to speak of the one who has died, and not feel that death is a subject never to be mentioned.

When a much loved husband or wife dies, the hurt cannot be healed quickly. The concern and caring of a devoted family will help, but a period of grief has to be endured. Indeed, it is harmful to try to hurry it or expect people to hide their natural feelings of sorrow. We need to mourn, and the happier the marriage the greater will be the pain of the one who is left alone. Family and friends are usually supportive at and immediately after the funeral, but it is in the weeks and months that follow that help is most needed. The death of someone we love brings a feeling of numbness and unreality at first. We cannot really accept that it has happened. As the weeks go by and the first shock passes loneliness can become unbearable. It is then that we most need the help and comfort of our friends.

However, although it may take time, even years, to recover from a bereavement, mourning should not be prolonged beyond its natural course, and we should not assume that we will never be happy again. We have a duty to others, as well as to ourselves, to try to rebuild our shattered lives and to start again on a new phase of our living. At some point we must decide that the time for grief is past, and we must set ourselves to put it aside and adjust to circumstances as they now are.

I am not suggesting at all that we should try to forget the one who has died. On the contrary, it is good to remember them, but in a more positive way and not with sadness. We can keep their memory alive and carry on the good influences which they were creating in their life time by seeking to continue the work which they began. If, for instance, they had been fond of the garden, to carry on making this as beautiful as possible would be fulfilling what they would have wished. If they had a special interest, hobby or charity which they cared deeply about, to devote time to this would be to advance what they had already started. I think that to do these things gives us the feeling that we are carrying out their own wishes, and can often bring them close to us. My mother loved gardening, and it was in the garden that I often felt very near to her after her death. Positive actions done in memory of people are far better than mere regrets for the past.

We cannot put the clock back or live again the years that are gone, but we can remember happy times with gratitude, and think of all the joys of years spent together. To have had a successful marriage is a wonderful privilege, and many have not known this blessing.

Time is needed to recover from sorrow; it is a slow and painful process. We have to be content merely to plod along at first, not expecting happiness, but just being determined to use life constructively. To be busy always helps. We should attempt to interest ourselves in a cause or charity, a hobby or pastime; preferably one which will take us into the company of others. Because we have known great sadness we will be able to understand the troubles of others, and in helping them will find solace ourselves. 'We cannot dry another's tears unless we too have wept' is a very true saying, and there are so many in need of our sympathy. It often helps to join an Association where others share similar problems. CRUSE (which is for widows and widowers) puts people in touch with each other, holds regular social gatherings and can give advice on legal matters etc.

For those who live alone, recovery is especially difficult. There is now no one to tell of the day's happenings, and it is so hard to return to an empty house. Sometimes it helps to get a cat or a dog for company. We need to be able to both give and receive affection, if only with an animal. A helpful book is *A Grief Observed* by C. S. Lewis, who describes how he coped with his own bereavement when his dearly-loved wife died.

Although familiar things about the house may bring back sad memories, it is not always wise to get rid immediately of all the deceased person's possessions. It is often very comforting to keep an article of clothing or some small treasure. It is better not to make decisions too soon, but to wait until the first state of numbness has passed, though belongings can be put out of sight for a while if this seems best. Similarly, no hasty decision about moving from the house should be made. While it is undoubtedly painful to be continually reminded of the loved one's presence, there will come a time when those same memories may be welcoming and comforting. It is usually advisable to wait for about a year before considering whether a change of home is desirable.

Finally, we should remember that the person who died would not wish us to remain unhappy for ever. They would be concerned and troubled by our prolonged grief, so for their sakes we should try to rebuild our lives and seek to be happy again. This is not in any way being disloyal to their memory. It is comforting if we hold the belief that death is not the end and that we shall, indeed, one day be with them again. I do not believe, myself, that life is snuffed out like a candle flame at death. I think it is only our bodies that die. When we come to think about it, even a candle flame goes on – the light from it travels out endlessly into space, even when it has been extinguished here. Edith Sitwell once wrote:-

> Love is not lost by death;
> Nothing is lost,
> Since all, in the end, is harvested.

## Separation and Divorce

After a divorce or separation the partner who is left can often suffer even more than if the marriage had been ended by death. In addition to the loneliness and sorrow, there are feelings of guilt and uncertainty. "Why didn't it work out?" "Was I to blame?" "Where did I go wrong?" If one partner in a happy marriage dies, the other can remember with gratitude their love for each other, and cherish those memories. The broken marriage leaves only bitter regrets and recriminations.

As in the case of bereavement, the isolated one often finds that friends tend to stay away at first, and as a single person it is difficult to fit in when other people are mostly in pairs. Learning to live independently takes a great deal of patience and adjustment.

Probably the most important thing is to keep fully occupied. If a paid job is not available, then voluntary work will certainly help to fill up the hours and give some purpose to living. It is best to take one day at a time; trying not to look back with regret to happier times in the past, nor fearfully into a future which seems bleak and empty. Circumstances change, and the pain will ease as the weeks go by.

If there are children, this will offset the loneliness, but will also bring problems of its own. Single parents do need the company of other adults from time to time. Fortunately, there are a number of clubs and associations which offer assistance, both to lessen loneliness and also to advise on the care of children. By enlisting their help the first difficult steps can more easily be made towards building up a new way of life.

# 3    The Loneliness of Old Age

"Grow old along with me,
The best is yet to be......"

So wrote the poet Robert Browning. Yet the thought of
growing old fills most of us with apprehension. We see old
folk in geriatric wards, lonely and with no interests to fill
their days; we see them in wheel-chairs, with hearing aids
and failing sight. As we grow older ourselves, we find that
we can no longer cope with the energetic activities of our
youth, we discover grey hairs, feel twinges of rheumatic
pain and imagine ourselves to be well on the downward
path to misery and decay. When Gustav Holst wrote his
composition "The Planets", Saturn was depicted as being
'the bringer of old age', and the music, although beautiful,
is a slow, sad dirge which seems to offer nothing but
hopeless desolation. Despite all this, I believe Browning to
be right. Life is a great compensator, and what is taken
from us on the one hand is usually restored on the other.

It is true that loneliness is most widespread among the
elderly. It can creep up on us as the years pass by, and we
no longer have the physical strength to make long journeys
in order to visit relatives or places of entertainment. Ill
health may confine us to the house, and even obtaining
necessary food becomes a problem, since few shops will
now undertake to deliver groceries to the door.

Some of these situations can be avoided if we take the
necessary steps. Local authorities will provide Home

Helps for the house-bound, and many Councils and organisations for the elderly have excellent schemes for assisting those in need. Rate rebates and grants are often available, and it is regrettable that many older folk do not realise this, or being fiercely independent, fail to claim the benefits to which they are entitled, preferring to struggle on unaided.

How can the traumas of old age be alleviated? Certainly, with advancing years, we shall no longer be able to lead the active life of our younger days, but many problems will no longer trouble us, for we shall have learnt from past experience to live at a more leisurely pace. For many, there will be the joy of grandchildren, and for those who can share their knowledge of life with the younger generation, being loved and needed within the family, loneliness will have no place, and to be old will assuredly not seem a time of loss.

But it is people living alone who fear most the passing of the years. It is all too easy to feel useless and unwanted. Nevertheless, there is a very great deal that older folk can contribute to a world in which pressures have built up and life must be lived at a breathless speed. Older people have that most precious of all commodities – time. Of course, time must be used; otherwise instead of a blessing it becomes a burden, and we are bored and oppressed by the tedious hours.

If we are in good health, we can try to involve ourselves in vountary work. There is plenty waiting to be done; we just need to find our own niche, whether it is taking library books to the house-bound, shopping for the disabled, helping in a play group or in a hospital canteen, or just visiting and chatting with someone else who is lonely. The hardest part is to get started; once we have done so, one thing will tend to lead to another, and before we know where we are we are fully occupied.

Even if we are shy and diffident about making this sort of contact with others, we can still find ways of using the time at our disposal. We can explore the world about us, learning more about birds, trees and flowers, or perhaps trying to write, paint or draw. We are never too old to learn. We can take a subject that interests us and find books about it in the library. Should we be completely immobile through illness or disability, we can still make use of our minds by praying for others who may be too involved in trials and troubles to pray for themselves. While life remains, there are always new ways of living it, new tasks to do, and new joys to be discovered.

A dealer once called at my mother's door asking if she had any antiques to sell. "I'm afraid not," said my mother, ruefully, "I'm the only antique here." But antiques are precious and much sought after. We should not under-rate ourselves just because we are elderly. In China and other Eastern countries the old are venerated because they have accumulated the wisdom of a lifetime. Their advice is sought and acted upon. Growing old should be a blessing rather than a bane.

> Let me grow lovely growing old,
> Old things are lovely too;
> Laces, ivory and gold
> And silks need not be new
> There is a beauty in old trees,
> Old streets a glamour hold.
> Why shouldn't I, as well as these,
> Grow lovely growing old?

So long as we are prepared to adjust as we go along, all will be well. The great thing is not to *feel* old. My aunt asked me one day to go with her to advise on the buying of a new dress. I pointed out one that I thought attractive. "Oh, no," my aunt said, "I couldn't wear that. It's an old lady's dress." She was then in her late eighties!

Age is a quality of mind.
If you have left your dreams behind,
If hope is cold;
If you no longer plan ahead,
If ambitions all are dead,
THEN YOU ARE OLD

But if you make of life the best,
And in your life you still have zest,
If love hold;
No matter how the years go by,
No matter how the birthdays fly,
YOU ARE NOT OLD.

If we look at an ancient oak standing proudly erect in the middle of a field, we can see how, over the years, it has grown sturdily and strongly in many directions and now supplies welcome shade for the cattle and supports much life in its branches, where birds nest happily and squirrels rear their young. After withstanding the storms of many winters, its roots are firmly and deeply established in the soil beneath. It is very different from the fresh and spritely young sapling, but it has a dignity and beauty of its own.

Perhaps the most important thing for us to remember as we grow older is that it is only our bodies that age. The young enjoy life through their bodily strength and the exuberance which they possess in such abundance: the old can experience an even greater joy through the wisdom, discernment and maturity of their minds. Here is a wise prayer for those who are ageing:-

Lord, Thou knowest better than I know myself that I am growing older, and will some day be old. Keep me from getting talkative, and particularly from the fatal habit of thinking I must say something on every subject and on every occasion.

Release me from the craving to try to straighten out everybody's affairs.

Make me thoughtful, but not moody; helpful but not bossy. With my vast store of wisdom it seems a pity not to use it – but Thou knowest, Lord, that I want a few friends at the end.

Keep my mind free from the recital of endless details; give me wings to get to the point.

Seal my lips on my many aches and pains. They are increasing, and my love of rehearsing them is becoming sweeter as the years go by.

I ask for grace enough to listen to the tales of others' pains. Help me to endure them with patience.

Teach me the glorious lesson that occasionally it is possible that I may be mistaken.

Keep me reasonably sweet. I do not want to be a saint; some of them are hard to live with, but a sour old woman is one of the crowning works of the devil.

Help me to extract all possible fun out of life. There are so many funny things around us, and I don't want to miss any of them. *Amen.*

# Positive and Negative Actions

## Loneliness in Youth

DO be prepared to spend time and trouble in talking and reading to a young child.

DO see that he has opportunities of meeting and befriending others of his own age.

DO consider taking him to a Nursery School or local Play Group.

DO find out about other suitable children's or youth organisations in your area.

DO encourage him to develop a hobby or special interest.

DON'T try to force children's friendships.

DON'T criticise a child or adolescent for failing to make friends, or make a great issue of it.

## Loneliness in Middle Age

DO seek advice if you have marriage problems. The Marriage Guidance Council have offices in most towns.

DO if you are left alone, find others in a similar position, by joining groups or associations for the single person.

DON'T   feel that life is over when your children leave home. It has merely entered a ncw phase.

DON'T   try to live in the past. Look at the present and prepare for the future.

## Loneliness in Old Age

DO      find out from the Social Services or Health Centre what help or benefits are available for you.

DO      look for new hobbies and interests that are within your capabilities.

DO      keep as fully occupied as possible.

DO      learn to come to terms with the limitations of age and discover its advantages.

DON'T   waste time in regretting the past.

DON'T   be afraid to ask for help if you need it.

DON'T   assume that you are useless. We can all do something.

# Part II
# States of Loneliness

Two conditions which are becoming increasingly common in these days of stress and strain are depression and agoraphobia. Both cause great distress to the sufferers and also to their families and friends, and by shutting people into themselves, are responsible for much misery and loneliness. Because they are serious contemporary problems and are much misunderstood, I shall devote this section of the book to explaining what depression and agoraphobia are and how they may be helped.

# 4 What is Depression?

Many years ago, the B.B.C. ran a radio programme known as "The Brains Trust". A popular member of its panel was a Professor Joad, and I remember how frequently he would reply, when asked to express an opinion on a controversial subject, "It depends on what you MEAN by that word." How right he was. The word depression does have more than one meaning. People often say, "Well, we all get depressed". That is certainly true, if by depression we mean that let-down feeling which comes when it rains heavily on the day we had planned a picnic, or we just miss a win on the Pools, or the money won't quite run to that holiday in Spain we had set our hearts on. But clinical depression is an entirely different matter. It is far more than merely a bout of low spirits, and is a real illness, not just a mood or state of mind.

The word depression literally means being pushed or pressed down, which quite neatly sums up the feelings of the depressed person. People sometimes say they have a sensation of heaviness, as if shackled to iron fetters. It can be described as the opposite feeling to that caused by the loss of gravity which astronauts experience in space where they have a sense of lightness and buoyancy. The depressed person finds that, for him, it is as if the gravitational pull has been increased, so that everything he does requires a far greater effort.

Imagine a pair of kitchen scales, the old-fashioned type with a scale pan on either side, which were used with brass weights. For accurate measuring both pans had to balance exactly so that they were on the same level. To be sure of good results, the cook was careful to balance all her ingredients accurately. Our lives are rather like this. Our conflicting emotions have to balance one another if we are to be fulfilled, efficient and happy. The brain, like the skilful cook, has to ensure this, by bringing into play the right responses to every situation in our lives. Sometimes this task becomes very complicated. Stresses and strains, worries and fears bring more and more emotions into conflict, so that it is hardly surprising when the brain is temporarily confused and gets the balance wrong. This is when tempers are lost or people become hysterical. If the excessive stress situation does not ease, a snowballing effect can take place, so that we over-react still further to bring yet more emotions into play until, in the resulting state of depression we are aware of bewildering sensations of fear, rage, shame and inadequacy, which by their very intensity reduce us to a condition of exhaustion. We wonder what is happening to us. Why are we acting so irrationally or inconsistently? We try to suppress or hide these feelings, and when that is no longer possible, to retreat into ourselves. It seems easier to remain at home, even safer to stay in bed; to try to opt out of an impossible situation.

But, except for a very small minority depression is a temporary state of mind. The brain has its own self-righting mechanism, and we can certainly help to hasten its progress. Unless we have been depressed from childhood, we can confidently look forward to the time when we will come out of our depression. Even for those whose depression will always be with them, there are now drugs which will enable them to lead a normal life. They keep the depression in check, just as insulin controls diabetes. So no-one need despair.

However, for most of us, it is just a question of going through the tunnel to find the light at the other end. But remember, the tunnel does have to be gone through. If we remain standing still we may see the light at the far end, but it will take us very much longer to reach it. We have to make an effort ourselves.

The symptoms of depression vary, but the most common are; exhaustion, despair, deep unhappiness, fear, a feeling of uselessness, guilt, anger and sleep problems. Most depressed people are ashamed of their feelings. They have always rather despised the hypochondriac, and depression can appear to be a form of this. Unsympathetic friends tell them to pull themselves together, to snap out of it, to think of others in far worse circumstances than themselves, and so on. The depressive simply cannot do this. With the best will in the world, it is impossible to think ourselves out of it.

Most people hate the idea of being 'a depressive'. Because it is an illness of the mind rather than the body, they fear it will lead to insanity, that they will not be responsible for their actions, or that their friends will regard them as being not quite right in the head. In fact, there is absolutely no reason to feel ashamed of this illness, or even particularly worried. While it is true to say that certain personality types are more vulnerable than others, the introvert or worrier being more likely to be afflicted than the extrovert, it can attack anyone at any time.

People sometimes become confused by the various medical terms which specify types of depression. They may be told that theirs is reactive, endogeneous, or manic; rather frightening names which suggest a serious condition. Doctors rarely speak of a 'nervous breakdown', though to the ordinary man or woman this aptly describes their condition. However, it is helpful to understand which particular form of depression we have and its probable causes. The main types are:-

### Reactive depression
This is by far the most common and, as its name implies, is caused by our reaction to adverse circumstances. The human mind and body are surprisingly resilient and can

endure long periods of pain, stress, anxiety and overwork, but there does come a time when some self-defensive mechanism in the brain seems to operate, switching us off as it were, so that we can no longer carry on with the same life style as before. The resulting depression slows us down, reduces our energy and makes it impossible for us to continue at the same rate. It can come about as a result of prolonged strain, after a series of severe misfortunes, or may follow a profound shock or traumatic experience such as a sudden bereavement. The duration of this sort of depression will depend on how long we take to adjust ourselves to a new pattern of living. Hurt minds need time in which to heal, and recovery must necessarily be a gradual process.

### Endogenous depression

There appears to be no obvious cause for this comparatively rare type. Sometimes sufferers feel that they have experienced it in some degree for most of their lives; indeed it may be that it has a genetic component. It can be treated, eased and cured in the same way as the reactive depression and, while it may not be possible for a complete cure to be guaranteed to everyone, most people with the right treatment are able to control their symptoms and live normal lives. Some doctors feel that endogenous depression is caused by an imbalance of certain chemicals in the composition of the body and that in time science will be able to find a way of correcting this.

### Post-natal depression

Sometimes it is known as 'baby blues' and is by no means uncommon. In fact, it is thought to affect as many as four out of every five mothers, especially following the birth of the first baby. Again it causes are not fully understood, but it is probably due to a combination of hormonal changes in the body, exhaustion and lack of sleep, anxiety or feelings of inadequacy, and changes in daily routine which caring for a new baby necessarily involves. In most cases the depression is only slight and will pass comparatively quickly, but if it is at all severe medical help should be sought because a mother can develop aggressive feelings or become obsessed with fears that she might harm or neglect her child. Midwives, social workers and other mothers can do much to help and reassure her, while husbands and grandmothers can certainly ease the problem if they are willing to shoulder some of the burden until she feels more able to cope alone. For the great majority of mothers, however, this depression will be only a minor inconvenience.

## Manic depression

This term is very often misunderstood and people have felt outrage and horror at being labelled a manic depressive. To most of us the word 'mania' suggests madness, but in this context it simply means that those who suffer from it experience swings of mood from manic (or high), when they are over-active and very excited, to depressed (or low), when they are plunged into inactivity and despair. These mood swings usually occur in regular cycles. Manic depressives need medical help which is different from that used in the other types of depression. They are usually given drugs which enable them to live their lives on a more even keel, reducing their activity to a normal level.

## Food and depression

Recent research has suggested that depression may be brought about as the result of allergic reaction to certain foods. While it is likely that only a few people are depressed as a direct result of eating any one particular food, it should be borne in mind as a possible cause and careful thought given to planning a healthy diet. Any suspect food may be eliminated for a trial period, provided adequate and properly balanced nourishment is maintained. If in doubt, a doctor or nutritionist should be consulted.

There are certainly some foods which appear to worsen depression and which should therefore be taken sparingly.

Strong tea or coffee and large amounts of alcohol are to be avoided. Caffeine, which is present in both tea and coffee, is a stimulant which lifts our spirits at first but, after a while, has a lowering effect. It is advisable to limit ourselves to three or four cups a day, using fruit juice or even water as healthier alternatives. Alcohol does bring temporary relief but, if we constantly turn to it as a means of escape, we risk adding alcohol dependency to the existing problem of depression. Chemical food additives are always suspect and it is best to use them as little as possible. Convenience or 'junk' foods may be quick to prepare but often provide little real nourishment. It is sensible also to reduce our intake of sugar, white flour, fat, salt and strong seasonings.

Other foods, however, are known to have a beneficial effect. Vitamins B and E, found in wholemeal bread and flour and in wheatgerm, help to give energy which we so often lack when we are depressed. Citrus fruit (oranges, lemons and grapefruit) blackcurrants, tomatoes, green vegetables and potatoes provide vitamin C, which is also essential for a feeling of well-being. It is all too easy when in a depressed state to make do with foods which take the least effort to prepare, existing, for example, on buns and cups of tea. This will only serve to prolong the depression.

It will be helpful now to consider some of the more common symptoms in greater detail, and ways in which they can be eased. But, before doing this, I should like to stress that any form of severe depression needs medical help. Considerable progress has been made in the study of anti-depressant drugs, and the doctor's advice should always be sought in the first instance. However, depressed people need a great deal of understanding, reassurance and after-care if they are to recover completely. I hope, therefore, to explain in the following pages how we can learn to control depression, and help both ourselves and others by understanding more fully what is happening to us in a depressive illness.

# 5  Common Symptoms of Depression

## Fear

One of the most common symptoms of depression is the feeling of fear. There is nothing wrong in being afraid at times. It is the normal reaction to any kind of threat, and triggers off the production of adrenalin in the body which gives us the extra energy either to run away, or to fight the challenge. But to live in a constant state of fear and apprehension is not natural, and it is this which leads to strain and exhaustion. In depression we are over-sensitive, and the least little worry or task provokes the sensation of fear and the feeling that we cannot possibly cope with it. The more depressed we are, the more inadequate and helpless we feel.

Depression takes away our natural defences; we can't shrug things off or laugh at them, we brood over chance remarks, we are exposed and vulnerable, and so we react by fear and withdrawal. Perhaps we wake in the morning and the thought of the tasks which lie ahead is so terrifying that we are afraid to leave the safety of bed. Or perhaps we make the effort to get up, and then dread parting from the familiar surroundings of the house. Other fears and phobias can develop, because events become magnified out of all proportion. It is as if our eyes see a spider, but our brain registers that we are being confronted by a menacing monster of twice our size from outer space.

These sorts of fears are rather like those of the small

child who does not yet understand the world he lives in and so cannot assess the degree of danger. That is why young children often fear the dark. It holds unknown terrors. I can vividly remember being lost at the age of about four, and feeling quite alone in an alien and hostile world. That feeling returned during my depression. I seemed to be completely isolated in the vastness of the universe.

Even if not actually living in fear, depressed people are in a state of continual anxiety. We just expect everything to go wrong. We lose all confidence in ourselves, and often put on an act, saying and doing the things we think our friends expect of us instead of acting naturally.

How can we get these fears and anxieties back into proportion? They are part of depression and will lessen as the depression heals. We have to work at it, but must not expect an instant cure; it will take time and patience. I can offer some suggestions, all of which helped me personally:

1.   Tackle each day just one of the things that you are afraid of. Attempt the least formidable first, and so long as you have achieved one victory only, you have made progress. Tomorrow you will be able to cope with something a little harder.

2.   Before tackling anything that frightens you, take a few really deep breaths. This has a surprisingly calming effect.

3.   Remember that if you have any religious belief, you are not really alone. I read once of a North American Indian tribal practice. At a certain age, a young boy had to spend the night alone in the forest on a moonless night. In the morning, when he had proved his courage, he would find that, unknown to him, his father had been keeping watch all night nearby to see that no harm befell him.

4.   Pretend that courage you don't feel and act a part. Your depression is fooling you by distorting your feelings. Try to think of it as an enemy, and concentrate on fooling *it*. Do you remember the old story of the traveller who saw

two lions blocking his path? He wanted to run away, but he kept on, and as he came closer he saw that they were chained and that he could safely pass between them.

5.    Finally, remember that people don't notice your reactions as much as you think. Most of them are coping with their own conflicting emotions. They too may be putting on an act of confidence. And don't worry if your progress is slow. If you have made any effort at all, YOU HAVE NOT FAILED. There is a wise saying, "It isn't the one who is beaten who fails, its the one who lies down". So, just think, "Well, I didn't manage it today, but at least I tried, and tomorrow I'll try again". Believe me, you will get there in the end, and when you do it's a wonderful feeling, like a boxer must experience after winning against terrific odds. After all, the harder the struggle, the more substantial the victory. If David had been as strong as Goliath, who would have thought him brave?

## Feeling useless

I think that most of us, in depression, feel that our lives are utterly and completely useless and futile. That is why some commit suicide; there seems to be no purpose in going on living. We must not accept these feelings as true, because our depression is misleading us and giving us a false picture.

Everything in life is either positive or negative, and when we speak of a balanced mind, we mean that we can distinguish between the two and steer a middle course through them. Think again of that pair of scales. When we are depressed, the weights are on the negative side, and we see only the bad and gloomy aspects of life. It is simply not true to say that anyone's life is of no account, whoever and whatever he is. I'm sure you know the quotation, "No man is an island". It is true. In some way or another we influence everyone with whom we come into contact throughout the day. The very depression which we hate so much in ourselves is possibly changing us, so that we will eventually have more understanding and compassion for others.

I have heard it said, 'People need people', and indeed we do all need to be needed. Because depression shuts us into ourselves we find it very hard to make contact with others, but this is what we have to try to do. Once we find that WE are needed, we shall know that we are not living useless lives. Those of us who are surrounded by family or friends will know already, except in our darkest moments, that we are needed in many ways, for we are part of our family's life. But those who live alone do not find it so easy to see a purpose in living.

When I was a teacher, I was once explaining to the children about electricity. I showed them how a bulb would only light up if the lead was touching the battery. Once it made contact, 'the magic' happened. In depression, we are like the bulb that has lost touch with the battery. We have to try to make contact again. I do know how hard this can be. A few years ago I found it almost impossible to keep up normal relationships with people, or even talk to them. However, if we are so shut into ourselves that we cannot reach out to others, or perhaps even leave our own home, some sorts of contact are still possible.

Growing and caring for a plant might be a first step. You are caring for something which is living and which is outside yourself, and this is the right approach. A pet, too, is a help, even if it is only a goldfish! Don't be afraid to ask other people for help, because it may help THEM to know that they are needed. Phone your friends, or write to them; anything to make a link. And have patience. Progress will be slow, but you will succeed in the end. So here are some things to aim towards:-

1.   Give care to something. It may be a plant, or an animal, or even a piece of furniture in the house that you can polish, or paint, or improve in some way.

2.   Make contact with someone by phone or letter. Don't forget that the Samaritans are always available by day or night.

3.   If you have any religious belief, try using the time which you have to spend alone in praying for others. This is a very positive action, and I believe that it can do a great deal of good.

4.   If you can knit, sew, cook, or construct things, there are plenty of charities which would welcome your talents.

5.   Remember that the greatest poets, musicians and artists usually suffered much personal unhappiness, and, in fact, it is probably because of this that they were able to produce such quality in the work they did. Many of them knew all about depression. So why not attempt to write a poem or paint a picture yourself? It doesn't matter in the least how bad it is. You don't have to show it to anyone! It is a way of expressing your feelings and frustrations and getting them out of your system.

I'm a very indifferent pianist; in fact it is so long since I tried that I probably could not play at all now, but in my teens I always played sad music if I felt miserable, and usually it had the effect of cheering me up.

It is important to keep reminding yourself that you are NOT useless. Someone has need of you, and there is a place in the world which you, and you alone, can fill. Even if you are temporarily out of action now, the time will come when you will be the one who is indispensable.

## Guilt

Feeling guilty, ashamed and blameworthy are also very common symptoms. All our feelings and emotions become magnified and distorted, and guilt is one of the most distressing of the unpleasant sensations that constantly nag at us. This consciousness of guilt is a negative thing. It saps our energy and does no good. How can we ease it? In the first place we must recognise that, for the most part, it is completely unnecessary. Much guilt is a burden which we load on ourselves with absolutely no justification. We look at others and feel that we should be achieving the same successes as them; we set ourselves impossible targets and then feel unworthy because we cannot attain them.

But the most common reason for the sense of guilt is the very fact that we find ourselves depressed. "What have you to be depressed about?" ask unsympathetic friends. "Look at old So-and-So, who is blind, deaf, badly housed, living alone (or whatever the case may be). HE isn't depressed. You should count your blessings." Now this is all very well, but the fact remains that you are NOT "old So-and-So", and you happen to have the illness called depression, which is no more your fault than it would be if you were to catch 'flu.

Sometimes, we feel that to give in to depression is a sign of weakness. This is simply not true. Have you ever tried to fight off a really bad bout of 'flu and pretend you haven't got it? I have, and landed flat on my back on the floor. Accept your depression, and accept treatment, and certainly don't blame yourself for your condition.

For those who have a deep religious belief, depression often brings guilty feelings. They think it must imply a lack of faith in God. Actually, I think this is very far from the truth. I do know that many of the clergy suffer from depressive illness. Some have felt that perhaps it is a testing time, and almost a privilege to be allowed to experience it. Certainly, once we come out on the other side, we can discover that it has not all been a waste. We become more understanding and more sympathetic to the problems of others. Gerald Priestland, a former Religious Affairs Correspondent for the B.B.C., said once, "The grey fellowship of the depressed is wider than it knows", (and he was speaking from personal experience). He quoted a nun as saying that she considered it to be the most revealing experience of her human existence. So I feel sure there is no need for guilt to have a part in our thoughts.

Another common cause for guilty feelings is after a bereavement. We regret that we had not done or said this or that for the person who is now beyond our reach. But, here again, I think we blame ourselves needlessly. We are all human; if we lived in complete harmony with one another at all times; if we never spoke a cross word, or made a wrong decision, it would not be life as we know it, and perhaps our very frailties make us better and more tolerant people.

I once possessed a very moral and Victorian game of 'Snakes and Ladders'. The board was covered in pictures; the snakes representing vices, and the ladders virtues. The interesting thing was that one thing led to another, with explanatory pictures at each end of the ladders or snakes. Greed led to sickness, kindness to friendship, and so on. Guilt, I remember, led to forgiveness; and this, I'm sure, is the right sequence. On its own, guilt is negative and destructive. Forgiveness brings healing. Very often, in depression, it is we who need to forgive ourselves. Look those feelings of inadequacy squarely in the face, realise your own humanity, and accept yourself as you are. This is the first step towards recovery.

Above all, we need to remember that everyone has some weakness or other. We have all, without exception, done or said things which we have afterwards regretted. Everyone has some sort of skeleton in the cupboard which we would rather no one else knew about. An old-time comedian once said that you have only to say to most people, "Flee, for all is discovered!" and they will at once panic. Perhaps that is rather extreme, but basically there is a lot of truth in it. So let us try to push away these unreasonable guilty feelings. They are symptoms of depression – no more than that.

## Sleep problems

Depression almost invariably affects our pattern of sleep. The two main problems are insomnia, or the desire for too much sleep. As insomnia causes the most distress, I will take this first.

You lie awake, the clock ticks on, and sleep refuses to come. The bed becomes more uncomfortable. You toss and turn, but you can't find an easy position. In the end it becomes intolerable to lie there. What should you do?

Let us consider the problem. We say, "I can't GO to sleep," as if we had to make a conscious effort to do it. In actual fact, this is not so. Natural sleep comes to US, and can easily take us unawares. Have you never nodded off while watching television, or felt your eyes shutting when sitting in a train or bus, or trying to concentrate on a boring speech or lecture? Why then does it not come at the proper time when we lie in bed at night? I think we prevent it ourselves by allowing our brains to be too active.

I formed the habit, myself, of working out the following day's programme, meals, or potentially difficult situations when I went to bed. It seemed the ideal time, when all was quiet and I was free of other distractions. The trouble is, that once the brain is stimulated into action, it is not so easy to switch it off. It moves from one subject to another, and sleep is pushed aside.

There are many ways of tackling this dilemma. Not all will work for you, but these general principles should be followed. There are things to consider during the day. Are you drinking too much tea or coffee? These stimulate the brain, and should certainly not be taken last thing at night if you have a sleeping problem. Try to limit yourself to four cups a day, but if you really must drink more than this, then keep it weak.

Take a little exercise just before bedtime; a brisk walk is ideal. Follow this with a warm bath and a soothing, milky drink. Don't eat a heavy meal very late in the day, but, on the other hand, don't go to bed hungry; either can keep you awake.

Now go to bed expecting to sleep. Make sure that the bed itself is comfortable and the bedding adequate but not too heavy, and also that you are warm enough. The room should be warm but not too stuffy. If you find complete darkness oppressive, try a night-light or low-wattage bedside lamp for company. Some people find that a cassette of very quiet music by the bedside will help them to drift off into sleep.

When you lie down, make up your mind to think of nothing. If thoughts and worries crowd in, either push them out by repeating a meaningless word over and over, (a modern variation of counting sheep) or imagine a large board with the word 'NO!' on it blocking out your thoughts, and concentrate hard on this instead. Then just relax and allow yourself to float into sleep.

If you still remain wide awake, get up for a while and sit in an easy chair with a book. Continue to read until you feel drowsy and your eyes are heavy. Then return to bed and you will probably drop off to sleep quite quickly.

However, if, despite all these efforts, you are still sleepless, do not worry about it. It is not so serious as you suppose. Your body will take that sleep if it really requires it. Think of how people have been tortured by being denied sleep. Their guards had to work really hard with bright lights and constant noise to keep their victims awake. I have heard soldiers describe how they had to snatch moments of sleep during prolonged battles and how they could sleep anywhere, despite discomfort, noise and danger when they really needed to. So, if you are lying awake, try to relax. Accept the situation and enjoy the feeling of just being still. Your body is resting, even if your mind cannot do so. You will almost certainly find then that sleep creeps up on you unawares.

Finally, if all else fails, the doctor may prescribe sleeping tablets. These are designed to correct the habit of sleeplessness established by your brain. As a temporary measure they are good, but we should not rely on them permanently. The quality of sleep they bring is inferior to natural sleep, and they usually make us feel heavy-headed the next day.

There are times, though, when depression takes us to the other extreme, and excessive sleep and continual weariness is the problem. We tire very early in the evening and are reluctant to get up in the morning. In fact, we are being driven to take refuge in sleep, so that the bed becomes a safe hiding place when life's stresses are too great. We must remember then, that once more, depression is deceiving us. Our bodies are not really so physically tired, and we should try to keep to a more normal bedtime routine.

Most doctors would agree that a proper sleep pattern comes as a result of peace of body and mind. To achieve this we need to feel content with our day's work, to have had adequate exercise, social contacts, and the knowledge that we are useful and loved. If these basic needs are satisfied it is almost certain that the sleep problem will no longer exist.

## Black Moods

A mood of black despair can descend on us with frightening suddenness and with devastating results. I was never much good at scientific subjects at school, but learning about stars and the planets always fascinated me. It seems that the more we find out about it, the more wonderful and amazing the whole universe is. Take black holes. Have you read about these? Apparently they are caused by something that is the opposite of an explosion; an *implosion*. It is like an explosion on a huge scale, but instead of everything being blown outwards, everything is sucked in, like water being drawn down the plug hole of an enormous bath. Black holes are far larger than the earth; they are strange and terrifying things. How do they get there? What causes them? Could we be sucked into one? No one really knows the answers. But scientists have hinted that, in some strange way, they might help in making future space travel possible. That in going through them, if that could be accomplished without being destroyed, we could go forwards or backwards in time. I don't understand it. As I said before, I am no scientist.

But don't you think that the expression 'black hole' describes what a mood of despair is like? It is certainly a hole. We fall down into it; and blackness is there too, and fear; the fear of being dragged into something terrible and unknown and being powerless to resist that dreadful downward pull.

Perhaps it will help us to remember that the black holes discovered by scientists make up part of our universe. We do not understand why they are there, but they play their part; perhaps, without them, the world and our lives could not have come into being. We do not really understand depression. It is always a frightening and can be a terrible experience; yet perhaps even depression has a purpose. Some doctors think it is the body's way of slowing down when pressures of life become too much for us. It is not usually a permanent state. We come through it and out on the other side. And when we do, we can use our experience and make something good of it. We can learn to accept life's ups and downs with more tolerance, and we can be far more sympathetic and understanding towards others who are finding life a struggle.

Fighting a black mood does not mean running away from it or pretending that it is not there. Nor is it forcing ourselves to do things which, for the moment, seem impossible. It is more like a cowboy riding a bucking broncho. To stay on its back needs all his efforts and he can do nothing else but concentrate only on this. He goes up and down with his steed, but he stays in control. If he should fall off, he does not give up. He remounts and tries again until the animal is mastered. This is how we fight depression. Go along with it. Don't worry that for the time being you can't cope with anything else. Ride it like the cowboy does and try to stay in control. You will master it in the end.

So, let us hold onto the thought that black moods can be overcome and need not destroy us. On the contrary, there may be a purpose in them; like those 'other black' holes they may be leading us on to something new and unknown and possibly beneficial to us.

# 6  Taking Control

There are many things that we can learn to do which will put us in the position of being able to control a depressed state and eventually to overcome it.

## Learning not to Procrastinate

"Procrastination is the thief of time", went the familiar Victorian proverb so frequently quoted to the young. When I heard it as a child, I had no idea what such an ominous-sounding word could mean. "It must" I thought, "be something particularly wicked." When I eventually discovered that it meant no more than postponing some duty or other, I was again fascinated by the way in which the word was built up, so that it literally means 'for tomor-rowing'; a very expressive way of describing what we all so commonly do. It is, of course, a very true saying; pro-crastination does indeed waste time, for as yet another proverb informs us, "tomorrow never comes".

I think that this habit of putting things off or delaying making any decisions is very much a sign of depression. Making a positive decision is very difficult when we are in this state. I can remember thinking about things which needed attention, worrying because they had not been done, and yet feeling quite incapable of tackling them. It was so much easier to think, "I'll do it tomorrow," rather like the small boy who prayed "God, please make me a good boy, but not just yet!"

When depression is severe, it seems less of an effort to go without a meal than to prepare it; even getting ready for bed can appear to be such a labour, that we grow more and more weary before we can bring ourselves to remedy it. Sometimes we worry so much over things left undone that this, in itself, increases the tension and anxiety we feel. Obviously it is the wrong attitude, but when we are so exhausted that everything that must be done takes a tremendous effort, how can we put the situation right?

I do understand very well the feeling of being under pressure because of all that has to be done. I tend to become flustered when work piles up, and feel that I just can't tackle it all. When there is too much, you simply don't know where to begin. Have you ever overslept and tried to hurry, only to find that you are dropping and losing things, falling over your own feet, and actually taking far longer than if you had carried on in the usual way? I think this is common to most of us. When I worked in an office I could not bear to see my 'In' tray full. In fact, I would either gaze at it in despair and feel it was quite impossible to cope with, or rush madly through the letters, probably doing them very badly, until it was empty, and then find myself wondering what to do next. I had completely wasted the energy spent in worrying that I should never get the work done in time.

I once met a man who gave me some very valuable advice about this. He was a storekeeper in a large firm. Once a year he had to do the stock-taking, a colossal job. He said that, at first, when he went into the storeroom and saw the utter chaos there, he used to feel that he didn't know how to start. But eventually he discovered the best way. "I go to one corner," he said, "and turn my back on the rest. I just get that corner straight and then work slowly backwards, and it's surprising how everything gets sorted out and the work done bit by bit."

This, I am sure, is how we should tackle a task which seems to daunt us. Don't give up in despair, but also don't try to do it all at once. Take one little bit, however small, and concentrate on that. Instead of worrying about how much you have to do and how difficult it will be, just try to make a beginning. Don't think of the whole job at all, but split it into fragments and take one at a time. It really is the best way to carry out most of the big things in life. If you feel that it is more than you can cope with, then by all means put SOME of it off until tomorrow, but not all of it. When you have done the little ration for today, you will have that much less to worry about tomorrow.

## Learning how to Adjust

We are creatures of habit. Life normally goes along, day by day, in more or less the same routine. We tend to be thrown out of gear when something happens to disturb this normal pattern. These sort of changes can often trigger off depression. The usual times of stress are in adolescence, the period following the birth of a child, the aftermath of divorce, separation or bereavement, during the menopause, after retirement and moving house. To these we must now add the all too common problems of redundancy and unemployment. Some of these events are natural and common to all of us; others are forced upon us by circumstances beyond our control. But each one can bring distress. So how do we cope?

The most important thing is to be as patient as possible, and not expect life to return to normal in a matter of days. After a period of strain a brief holiday will often work wonders and give renewed energy to deal with the situation when you come back to it.

It always helps to look ahead and make sensible preparation beforehand. This does not mean anticipating something like the menopause with apprehension and worrying about it, but it does mean deciding what practical things to do should the need arise. It is, for example, advisable to plan for retirement several years ahead of the time, listing the new hobbies and ventures you will have the leisure to pursue, and reading the various books and pamphlets available on this subject. Some local authorities run pre-retirement courses. Similarly, a move to a new house is much less traumatic if cupboards and drawers are gone through well in advance, things not needed thrown away, and those not in daily use packed up in cartons, and lists of jobs to be done written out. The *Which?* book, *Which Way To Buy, Sell, And Move House* gives excellent advice and can be thoroughly recommended as a guide.

As far as the menopause is concerned, I think many women worry unnecessarily. Most experience only minor discomfort. In any case, doctors have now discovered a simple hormone treatment which will alleviate any real distress. So the answer, if you have problems at this time, is to visit your G.P.

For the divorced or separated I can recommend the booklet *Alone Again* published by the Marriage Guidance Council. A very helpful leaflet for the bereaved, "Easing Grief For Oneself And Other People" is obtainable from the Relaxation For Living Association. There is, I am afraid, no easy solution for those trying to cope with redundancy and unemployment. I can only say that we can make the best of the situation by trying to adjust ourselves slowly and by living only one day at a time. It is really a question of using the resources and materials we have at the present. They may not be what we would have chosen for ourselves, but it is up to us to make what we can of them.

This quotation may be helpful to keep in mind if you are going through a period of change and instability:-

> One day at a time; this is enough. Do not look back and grieve over the past, for it is gone; and do not be troubled about the future, for it has not yet come. Live in the present, and make it so beautiful that it will be worth remembering.

## Learning not to Look Back

When I was teaching, and the children in my class were practising races for their Sports Day in the summer, I always told them that it was most important to run straight on and not look back to see if anyone was catching them up. "It could lose you the race," I told them, "because looking back slows you up." Sometimes I reminded them of the old Greek story of Orpheus and the beautiful maiden Eurydice. He went to rescue her from the Underworld, where she was held a prisoner, and was told that he might lead her out, providing he did not look back. They survived the long and difficult journey, but Orpheus, as he emerged into the light of day, looked back to see if she too was safely out. Alas, she had not quite reached the entrance, and so was lost to him for ever. These old myths contain valuable truths. That is why they have survived for so long, and we can see the wisdom of their teaching. It is a human weakness to want to look back at the things which are past; to cling to them and try to bring them forward into the present.

When we are depressed, it is all too easy to remember past days when we were happy, and long to return to them. Childhood memories tease us; life seemed so different then, and the world so much more joyous a place. As we grow older we may have to face bereavement. How natural it is to yearn to be once more with those we have lost. Often we find a move to a new area upsetting; we feel it has been a mistake, and we remember the old familiar places with regret and nostalgia.

It is important to realise, though, that these are all negative feelings. Negative feelings will only increase and intensify depression. We know very well that we cannot 'put the clock back' or live in the past. Yet how hard it is not to long to do so, especially when we are feeling low.

When these thoughts come, we should try to do two things. First, to bear in mind that life is rather like an escalator; it goes on moving continuously, and we must go with it, whether we wish to or not. The second is that it is not the fact of thinking about the past that is harmful. Memories can be used for good, but only if we can remember the past with gratitude; not with resentment because it HAS passed. We have gone on, our time is here and now; but it is possible to make the present happier if we can bring past pleasures back to mind without wanting to return to them. Wordsworth did this when he recalled the host of daffodils he had once seen dancing under the trees. The memory gave him pleasure every time he brought back that little bit of the past into the present. The mistake we so often make is to reverse the process and try to escape back into the past.

I suppose the most vivid example of the dangers in trying to return, is the story of Lot and his wife escaping from the doomed town of Sodom, and she, remembering regretfully former pleasures there, lingered to see what would happen and was, presumably, caught in a rain of volcanic ash and, as the Bible says, "turned into a pillar of salt". I was frequently told, as a child, to "remember Lot's wife", and I'm sure it was good advice.

I am convinced that looking back, if it is with regret, is negative and can only hurt us. We cannot alter or bring back the past; we CAN shape the present and the future.

## Learning to Ride the Storm

Perhaps because I live near the sea, I have sometimes thought of life as a voyage, with myself as the captain in charge of my body, the ship. I see depression as a passage through particularly dangerous and stormy waters; a challenge such as the rounding of Cape Horn would have been in the days of the old brigantines. The captain of any small craft knows only too well that you cannot sit passively through a storm. You fight it tooth and nail, setting or hauling in the sails according to the wind, securing your valuable cargo, and so on. If the storm continues you may have to go with it, after making sure that all reasonable precautions have been taken, and ride it out. Nevertheless, you remain vigilant and wide awake, lest the wind drives you too far off course or onto hidden rocks. It is true that some ships may be lost at sea, but the more responsible the captain, and the more skilled he is in seamanship, the more likely it is that his vessel will survive. He will have seen to it that the ship is seaworthy and in good repair; that his instruments, and in particular the compass, are in working order, and that he himself is aware of the positions of dangerous rocks or currents to be avoided at all costs.

When we compare a ship battling through a storm to a person struggling to overcome depression, we can find many similarities. As the captain is aided by his compass, we may be helped by having an aim in life; something which lies on the other side of the depression, and on which we can fix our sights; the light, perhaps, which we believe to be at the other end of the tunnel. Then, however stormy the weather, we shall reach our destination.

> One ship sails east, and another sails west,
> While the self-same breezes blow.
> 'Tis the set of the sails,
> And not the gales,
> That bids them where to go.
>
> And directing our course is the power of faith,
> As we journey our way through life.
> 'Tis the set of the soul.
> That decides the goal,
> And not the storms and strife.

A ship has to be kept in good repair if it is to withstand the rigours of a voyage. We too need to ensure that we are not weakening our bodies, as so often happens in a period of depression, by neglecting to eat proper food, having insufficient sleep, or taking too little exercise.

There are many rocks to be aware of. Suicide is the most obvious, but there are also the risks of trying to find relief in the excessive use of drugs or alcohol, or in giving up the struggle by retreating into ourselves in an attempt to opt out of life.

Finally, it may be encouraging to reflect that a ship's owner would obviously look for a good captain before sending his valuable ship through perilous seas. Such a captain, having successfully completed a difficult assignment, would be proud of his achievement in overcoming the elements, and would have added still further to his skills by doing so. Might it not be that going through depression is a gainful experience, making us more mature, more tolerant, and more considerate towards our fellows? No sailor, of course, would choose to encounter storms, and how simple life would be if it was always a voyage over calm and sunny waters; but true seamanship can only be learned outside the safe and pleasant harbour.

When I was teaching, I discovered that children learn far more by doing and experimenting than by passively listening; and in life's school I am convinced that we learn by all our experiences, whether pleasurable or painful. Only by living through them can we develop our personalities to the full. It is hard to understand the reason for suffering and pain; we feel that we could have made the world so much better, had we been in charge of its creation. But would our perfect universe really have been a happy place? Happiness does not automatically follow the gratification of all our desires. Without the experience of grief and distress, could mankind have developed the ability to feel wonder, sympathy, gratitude, kindness and love? Might not our paradise eventually have become peopled with a self-satisfied, selfish, feeble and utterly bored race of men and women?

# 7 Hope

Hope is the one word, more than any other, which we must hold on to if we are to emerge from depression; its opposite, and the one which we must turn our backs on, is despair. When we are in the midst of any great distress, it is almost impossible to believe that the existing state of affairs will ever change. People say, "It will pass", "Time is a great healer", and all the other glib phrases, but they simply do not ring true. We are experiencing the present grief and pain, and our minds can register only this.

But hope is rightly named one of the three great virtues. It is the very best antidote to depression, in fact it can be said that depression is the loss of hope. We feel, "What's the use of living?, what have I to look forward to?, what use am I?, what's the good of doing anything?". Our depression is deluding us, tricking us into these feelings of hopelessness that are simply not justified. Hope is not really lost. We must just hang on to it and go on believing that it is there, despite all apparent evidence to the contrary.

You may know the famous painting of Hope by the artist Watts. In it a woman is shown sitting blind and alone on top of an empty world. She holds a lute, of which all but one string is broken, and she listens to the faint tune it can play, the only thing that is left to her. But she still hopes. She believes that everything is not lost, and that good will eventually come.

An abstract word like hope is difficult to define. Perhaps

'light' is the best metaphor we can make of it. When we cannot sleep we long for the dawn; pain seems easier to bear, and fears less frightening during the daylight hours.

I remember vividly a visit I made many years ago to a small coal mine in Lancashire. In the labyrinth of narrow, underground tunnels, our little party stumbled along over the uneven floor, thankful that our heads were protected by helmets from the rocks jutting from the low roof above. It occured to me how terrible it would be to be lost down here alone, and how infinitely more terrible to be lost without a light, because, apart from the powerful torches fixed in our helmets, the mine was in total darkness. During my time of depression, I felt very much in that very situation; groping my way through a dark tunnel, lost and afraid. But there was hope: the belief that somewhere ahead the tunnel would end and there would be light again. By holding fast to that hope, it is even possible to find something good in depression while it is still with us.

The sun, as a bringer of light, is often a symbol of hope. Do you know the Flanders and Swann song deploring the British climate? They take the months, one by one, and point out all the dismal weather prospects. Even for July, they can only say,

> In July the sun is hot:
> Is it shining? No, its not!

How typical this is of depression. We feel that the sun has disappeared and gloom has descended permanently. It seemed to me that I carried round my own personal black cloud over my head!

And yet, the amazing truth is that, even in winter when the skies are overcast and the nights long and dark, the sun is still in its place in the sky. It's position is unaltered; it is only that the earth has turned away from it. We know this, of course, but primitive people used to fear that the life-giving sun had deserted them for ever, and winter became indeed a time of fear and dread. That sort of fear returns in depression; we feel that the darkness of our minds is permanent.

Bishop George Appleton described it well. He said, "Depression can be like a dark cloud descending on one". But he went on to remind us that a cloud can be penetrated. He tells us to remember that "an aircraft on a rainy day rises through dark clouds to the brightness of the sun, and as we look down on the clouds beneath, they are seen as bright, rather than as dark and gloomy, in unending horizons of bright sunshine". Hang on to the knowledge that you, one day, will see your depression like this.

I read a science fiction story once in which all the people, because of some disaster on earth, had lived for generations in deep caverns underground. Because there was no light they had become blind. Their folklore held stories of light and sunshine, and they had come to think of the sun as a sort of god. But it was no longer real to them; only a part of their children's world fantasy, and most of them denied its existence. Yet all the time, above their dark and dismal caves, the sun blazed out in all its glory.

We are sometimes like this when we are caught up in fears and anxieties, or when we feel that atomic war, or famine, or pollution will destroy the world, or that we ourselves are useless and life pointless. When we are depressed these negative feelings intensify and torment us. My own belief is that good, like the sun, is always there, even if temporarily hidden from us, and that the things which really matter go on for ever, even through death. An old verse says, very truly I think:-

> Beauty, strength, youth are flowers, but fading seen;
> Duty, faith, love are roots and ever green.

I also came across these words about hope, written by Wilfred Peterson. "The well-known maxim, 'While there is life there is hope' has deeper meaning in reverse – 'While there is hope there is life.' Hope comes first, life follows.

Hope gives power to life. Hope rouses life to continue, to expand, to grow, to reach out, to go on. Hope sees a light where there isn't any. Hope lights candles in millions of despairing hearts. Hope is the miracle medicine of the mind. It inspires the will to live. Hope is the physician's strongest ally."

But how can we find hope when we are depressed? When a particularly black mood descended on me one day, with its usual unexpected suddenness, the thought came to me that I could perhaps use this experience. One day; certainly not at that time when I felt incapable of any positive action, but one day, when I was well again, I would use the depression and take advantage of it. Now I understood what it was. I had felt it and lived with it, so I might be able to help others who were trying to escape from its snares. The thought alone reduced my depression that day, and I knew then that this was the way to fight it; to look it in the face, think of it as a menacing evil and say to it, "Right! Come and do your worst and I will still make some good out of you." This, I think, is what is meant in the Bible by the "treasures of darkness". Robert Browning expressed a similar thought when he said:-

> Then welcome each rebuff
> That turns earth's smoothness rough,
> Each sting that bids nor sit, nor stand, but go!

There will always be ways in which the experience gained in depression can be put to use in later life.

A friend of mine, who was training to be a missionary, would always shrug off any set-back or annoyance by saying, "Oh well, it's all G.M.T." When I asked what she meant she said, "It's just that a missionary may be sent anywhere, perhaps to a primitive race where she could be called upon unexpectedly to help in any situation, from delivering a baby to digging a well. We have to regard ANY experience we may have as 'good missionary train-ing', or G.M.T." Perhaps it would help us if we could think of our trials and tribulations, even depression, as G.L.T. – 'good life training'!

And here are three more practical suggestions:-
1.  Do something positive. So long as you are taking some sort of action or effort, you are working towards a better time ahead.
2.  Hope for the moment. If you can see no good in the future, just live for today. Look forward to the next good thing, however trivial; a hot meal, a book to read, a television programme, the warmth of a fireside chair, the knowledge that tonight the stars will shine and tomorrow the sun will rise.
3.  Believe in hope. Through the ages man has lived by hope. Without it we should still be animals, just accepting our surroundings and making no attempt to reach out to better things. So, if you believe that your depression will pass, you will be on the way to escaping from it.

What we must do is to go on looking up and forward; never down and backward. The option is ours:-

Two men looked out through prison bars,
One saw mud: the other stars.

# 8   Taking Action

In working to control and overcome depression, it is very necessary to take as much positive action as we can manage. As in any other illness, the will to be well is vital to the cure. All the following will help us.

## Medical Care

This is the first and most important consideration. No-one who is seriously affected by depression should try to struggle on alone without the doctor's help and advice. I am not suggesting that this will merely mean taking tranquillisers and sleeping tablets. The depressive is usually lethargic enough. But a doctor will be able to assess the degree of depression and decide whether anti-depressant drugs are needed, or perhaps other specialised treatment. Some people refuse to take any drugs at all, and this, in my opinion, is ill-advised. In depression the brain patterns are disturbed. The same thing happens in severe insomnia; the pattern of sleep is broken, and by taking sleeping tablets for a brief period, the right rhythm is once more restored, after which the tablets are no longer needed. Anti-depressant drugs correct the working of the brain in a similar way, making it easier and quicker for the patient to return to a more normal state of mind.

It is necessary to point out that these drugs may have side-effects; what suits one person may upset another, as I myself learnt. Some preliminary trial and error may be experienced, but once the proper remedy is discovered, it can be a tremendous help, and these drugs, unlike some tranquillisers, are not addictive or harmful in any way. Most people will need drugs for a short time only, but in a few cases of severe depression they may have to be continued as a permanent treatment. Even so, this need be no great hardship, for it is then possible to lead an almost normal life, just as the diabetic, by taking insulin regularly, is enabled to do. But, for the vast majority of sufferers, depression will eventually pass.

## Making Our Thoughts Positive

When we are depressed, our thoughts tend to get into a kind of rut. We think in a negative way. If we try to analyse our thoughts, we find that we are continually feeling, 'I can't. I'm a failure. How terrible the news/weather/my health/looks etc. are. Today I've got to cope with . . . . . . and I'll never do it. It's no use trying. I'm so frightened! . . . . . . and so on. We are obviously getting things out of proportion; putting them the wrong way round. But how can we get our minds back on to a more positive track? It is not easy, but this, I would suggest, is how to tackle it. It can only be done gradually, and is an uphill struggle, rather like trying to drive the car with the brake on. But it *can* be done.

You must work at it all the time, trying to do at least one positive thing each day. It helps to keep a record and write down your daily achievements. You might begin when you wake in the morning, by thinking of all the enjoyable things that the day has in store (even if it is only something nice for lunch!) Perhaps you can think of nothing pleasant at all. Well, never mind. Try looking in the newspaper and find something good there. In spite of what people say, the news is never wholly bad. When you find a good news item, spend some time in thinking about it.

If that fails, go out of doors and find something

beautiful; perhaps a tree, a flower or a cloud, and look at it and try to appreciate it. This works for me, because I was in danger of losing my sight at one time, and now I can certainly feel thankful for being able to see. Think of something you normally enjoy when you are not depressed; books, music, a television programme or a hobby, perhaps; knitting, cooking, swimming, cycling, or whatever it may be; and then, even if you have no real inclination to, make the attempt to do it. Very often you will find that the enjoyment will come back once you have started.

To do anything at all is a positive action. When we are badly depressed we usually want to do nothing. We stay in bed, or sit and stare into space. Remember that the feeling of bodily exhaustion is largely an illusion. Once we start to do something it often wears off. So any sort of doing is a way of overcoming depression.

Even a smile is a positive action. I used to draw myself a card like this:-

and carry it around with me, to remind myself to smile more frequently at the children in my class at school. I felt that they, poor mites, all too often saw me looking like this:-

So here is an aim: first smile yourself, if you can, then as the next step, try to get someone else to smile at you. Make a pleasant remark to the postman, check-out girl, or bus driver and give yourself a mark on your record when you achieve it. It is not easy. I know how hard it can be. I always found it a real effort to speak to people; my brain just seemed to go numb. I am quite sure, though, that this is how to fight depression.

## Companionship

It is very difficult for the depressed person to make contact with others, and yet this can be vital. Loneliness can trigger off depression and certainly make it worse. Sometimes friends are unsympathetic or impatient, and even if they want to help, it is easy to feel that we are burdening them with our constant misery. This is where organisations like the Samaritans are so valuable, and even more so the self-help groups of fellow depressives, where people can meet each other and gain mutual support.

## Keeping Busy

It is important to be fully and gainfully occupied. Daily work, and even former pleasures, have probably become a burden, but those who have a hobby should spend a little time on it each day. Even if the inclination is not there, which is more than likely, the enthusiasm will gradually come back. A hobby often expresses and develops our personality, and the loss of interest in it shows the devitalising character of depression.

## Exercise

Medical tests have shown that exercise stimulates certain hormones in the brain which counteracts depression. Any form of exercise is beneficial. Most people feel a lack of energy, and are unable to participate in the more strenuous sports, but a little gentle walking, gardening, swimming or cycling should be attempted. It is definitely harmful to stay indoors day after day, and this should be avoided if at all possible. There is far more of interest to be found out of doors where events are happening, people to meet, and new and sometimes unexpected occurrences to act as a diversion.

# Horticultural Therapy

The expression may sound somewhat grand, but it simply means gardening, caring for indoor plants, or indeed cultivating any sort of plant or herb. The coming of spring, even for those who are shut into the centre of the most dingy and built-up city, always seems to make its presence felt. There is a different atmosphere, and we can almost sense new life stirring in trees and bushes, the sky looks clearer, bird song starts at the earliest light, and, or so they say, "a young man's fancy lightly turns to thoughts of love".

But sadly, in depression, all this passes us by. It is as if we are only half alive. I think that by putting ourselves into closer contact with growing things, as we do in gardening, we can sometimes feel in tune again with the life around us.

For those who enjoy plants and flowers, this sort of therapy can be well worth trying. When we are depressed we do not want to make the effort to do even those things which gave us pleasure in the past. It might be worth attempting, just for a short time, and give Nature a chance to work the cure; to potter in the garden for a while, or take a really close look at those new leaves and flowers. There is something beneficial which is derived from actually touching and handling earth and plants: somehow we then feel ourselves a part of the living universe. But, if you feel that even this is too much for you, or if you have never done any gardening before, start in a very simple way by growing some cress seeds indoors on a piece of wet lint in a saucer. It couldn't be easier, and from that you can progress to growing other plants or seeds.

Do try a little horticultural therapy. It could be the cure you are seeking, or at least the beginning of it.

## Self Esteem

I love me, I love me,
I love myself, I do . . . . . . .

went an old Music Hall ballad. Few depressives would agree with the song writer. When we are depressed we come nearer to hating than loving ourselves. "I'm a failure." "My life is worthless." "There must be something wrong with me." "I'm one of those awful depressed people." "I mustn't let anyone know what I'm really like, or they'll despise me." "Why am I so inferior to everyone else?"

How often we have thoughts like these, and they are a sure sign of depression. It is again a question of getting the balance right. I am not proposing that we should aim at being big-headed and conceited. That would be to go to the other extreme. A well-balanced person keeps to the midway course, and that is how it should be.

It is seldom wise to compare ourselves with others and try to become exactly like them. The astonishing thing about human beings is that out of all the millions of us in the world, not one is an exact replica of another. We all have our own characters, and we all have a unique place to fill. Every part of our nature fits us for that position, and if we try to put ourselves elsewhere we become round pegs in square holes. So, maybe we cannot swim the Channel, win a beauty contest, get on to the board of managers, drive a car or what have you; but there is something that we can do or be which no one else in the whole universe can. I came across an old gypsy saying once:- "Never laugh at someone who is not as clever as you, for each one knows something that you do not know."

A sense of inferiority is not necessary. It is the depression which takes away our feelings of security and confidence and which makes us doubt our own abilities and worth. The way to fight off those feelings is to try to respect and live up to the best that we can be and then, when we have done that, to accept ourselves as we are. We should never need to feel that we must apologise for being ourselves. It was Shakespeare who said:-

> To thine own self be true,
> And it shall follow, as the night the day,
> Thou canst not then be false to any man.

In fighting depression it is vital to "know the enemy." It is very discouraging to find that after several days when the black cloud has lifted, it suddenly returns with renewed intensity, like a crafty foe waiting for a chance to stab his victim in the back. This is only to be expected, for this is the nature of depression. The way out is, almost always, two steps forward and then one back. The attacks will lessen in frequency and severity until it finally does go. Often too, it can cause physical aches and pains which are by no means imaginary and can be very severe, but which have originated from the mind rather than the body.

To explain the characteristics of depression to those who had never experienced it themselves I sometimes found it helpful to remind them of the Hans Anderson story of "The Snow Queen". In this tale, minute fragments of an evil mirror were scattered over the world, and found their way, unnoticed, into people's eyes and hearts. This distorted their vision and their thoughts to such an extent that everything they saw appeared to be ugly, twisted and drab, while they themselves grew cold, withdrawn and unresponsive. The effects of depression are rather like this, giving the illusion of a grey, hostile world, and suppressing and inhibiting the normal feelings and emotions of its victims. Just as positive action is need to remove a foreign body from the eye, so we have to make the effort required to rid ourselves of depression.

# 9 Relaxation

In the previous chapter I discussed ways of fighting depression by taking positive actions. All these ways will indeed help to shorten the duration of a depressive illness, though I must add a warning that the cure will take time. Patience and perseverance are very necessary. To go on, now, to recommend relaxation may seem rather a contradiction. However, while our minds must be stimulated to take a positive attitude in order to overcome the lethargy which inhibits our thoughts and actions, we must, at the same time, learn how to relax the tensions which depression builds up in our bodies.

Sometimes, when digging in the garden, I have disturbed an ants' nest. I have watched, fascinated by the commotion this has caused. Ants rush frantically hither and thither in an apparently mindless confusion.

I have often thought that depressed people are rather like this. I used to feel that I had a tremendous burden of work to do and would struggle hard at it all day, and yet seem to have achieved next to nothing. At other times, I was quite incapable of physical effort and would just sit passively, yet I would feel my mind whirling round as if it were trying in vain to sort itself out. This state of turmoil comes about because, in depression, we are being bombarded by so many sensations of fear, guilt, frustation, loneliness and misery, that they become mixed together into a meaningless jumble.

We should not be afraid of these feelings. They are only

a part of the illness, and it is not uncommon for ill-health to produce symptoms of this kind. A person with a high fever will toss and turn and perhaps become delirious as the brain is over-stimulated. In normal health, we are able to control our activity to the correct degree. We find that it is possible, even in stressful situations, to switch off completely and to be still. In Nature, when storms come, plants and trees that stand stiffly are broken; those that bend and accept the wind are unharmed when the sunshine returns. We must try to accept our troubles, letting them flow over us and believing that better times will come.

I can recall, as a child, gazing awe-stricken at the Big Dipper in Battersea Park Fairground in London. The cars hurtled down from terrific heights at a breakneck speed, and the shrieks of the passengers hardly suggested that it would be a joyride. My sister, however, persuaded me to venture aboard and showed me the technique. "Go with it," she said. "When the car goes over the top and plunges down steeply, lean forward and become part of the momentum; when it is climbing up and slowing down, lean back and relax." It really worked. I enjoyed that ride. I went with it and yet I was in control, and at the end of the trip I alighted, having both enjoyed and learned from the experience.

Recently I went into a busy office where two counter clerks were dealing with long queues of customers. Suddenly phones rang simultaneously behind each of them. Neither became flustered. They continued to deal quietly with the person who required their attention, until they could conveniently turn aside to answer the telephone. This is the right way to deal with stress.

In the 1940's, there was a popular radio programme entitled "In Town Tonight". It began with the confused roar of traffic, mingled with the shouts of street-market sellers and the sounds of the milling crowds. Then abruptly, as a voice shouted STOP! all the noise ceased. Similarly, if we can discover the right way to do it, we need to be able to switch ourselves off from the stresses and strains of life.

We need to learn again the value of stillness, tranquillity and inner peace. For bodily relaxation I can recommend breathing exercises and the technique of breath control. This can do a great deal to relieve nervous tension. Sometimes we can increase stress by trying too hard to fight it. I once heard of a woman who asked the help of a priest because she seemed to be unable to pray. She had tried desperately, but felt there was a barrier between herself and God. The priest said to her, "YOU are building the barrier. Go home. Go into your room, shut the door, sit down on a chair and DO nothing. Think of nothing, say nothing; simply be still. And, whatever you do, don't try to pray. Let peace come to you."

I have been reading about hurricanes, and it is amazing that in the very centre of those terrible, mad whirlwinds there is an area of complete and utter calm, known as the eye of the storm. Specially equipped planes are able to break through the outer turbulence and enter this quiet space. Perhaps we do not realise that we all have within ourselves a centre of calm, however disturbed our minds may seem to be. The poet Browning wrote: "There is an inmost centre in us all, where truth abides in fulness."

I have, for my part, found that the easiest way to learn relaxation is to consider beauty in any form; music, nature, poetry or art, whichever has the most appeal. I was once told that when springtime comes in Japan and the parks are full of flowering trees, you will frequently see little groups of people sitting under the blossoms just gazing up and enjoying the beauty of it. We should think it odd: we all too often rush past and take it all for granted.

It is however, really worth preserving these pictures in our minds. Minds are rooms which need furnishing, and we each choose our own decor. Why opt for a room as bare as a prison cell? Wordsworth had his picture of the daffodils. I too have a Lake District picture, for once, on holiday there, I stopped to marvel at the effect of the evening light over the fells. It was as if my mind took a photograph of the scene without my being aware of it, and I still have it whenever I want to recapture that moment. The same thing happened once when I looked up through masses of pink cherry blossom to the clear blue of an April sky. These pictures surpass any painted by a human artist. So, when I was depressed, I would sometimes think of these; or I would take a flower and bring it indoors and look at it, trying to appreciate its perfection. At other times, I would play some favourite music, and try to let the composer fill my mind with his thoughts rather than my own.

I heard a broadcast recently by a blind girl who had unexpectedly regained her sight. She could not understand how others were so unmoved by the beauty around them, she could only marvel at what she saw. W. H. Davies most truly said,

> "What is this life, if full of care
> We have no time to stand and stare?"

# 10   Sharing the Burden

One of the worst effects of depression is the sensation of being trapped inside oneself in a condition which is incomprehensible to others, and the resultant feeling of isolation can be very distressing. This is why self-help groups, where depressives are encouraged to meet one another, can provide a great deal of relief. A friend once told me that just the realisation that such a group existed, and that others could understand and care about her problems, was in itself enough to bring great comfort. Those who have known depression themselves are certainly qualified, by their own experience, to advise and help other sufferers, and can provide fellow depressives with companionship, sympathy and moral support.

It is a false argument to say, "I have too many troubles of my own to take on other people's". A traveller in Africa noticed that his native bearers made use of a long pole when carrying his heavy equipment. The men invariably chose to carry two objects rather than one, for when tied to each end of the pole, the weights balanced one another and made the load easier to carry.

There is a Chinese legend which tells of a wise man who was, as a special privilege, allowed to visit both Heaven and Hell. Hell, he was surprised to see, was a most beautiful place where food was in abundance, but its inhabitants tormented, because they were only permitted to eat it with chopsticks six feet in length, and so were quite unable to convey any of the food to their lips. When he was conducted to Heaven the wise man saw an equally beautiful place, with the same delicious food plentifully provided. Here the people were happy and contented. "I suppose the six foot long chopsticks are not required in this realm", he observed. "On the contrary", he was told, "the same rule applies; but here the people are those who have learnt to feed each other. So all are satisfied and have everything they could wish for."

The urge to retreat into our own shells is harmful and we should try to resist it by attempting to meet, and if possible do things for others. In helping them we will help ourselves even more. If we live alone, we should endeavour to go out as much as possible. Depression is always worse if we stay confined to the house. It is good to develop hobbies and interests to keep ourselves busy. In the periods when the depression lifts, we can immerse ourselves in these and it will help to keep it at bay. We should not complain that people never come to visit us. They never do if we wait for them. We have to take the initiative, however hard that first step may be. Remember, people need people. Once we begin to reach out to others the isolation is broken.

# 11    The End of the Tunnel

Anyone who has emerged from a period of depression can appreciate the old story of the man who continually banged his head against a wall, and when asked why he was doing it, replied "It is such a wonderful feeling when I stop!" Not much can be said in favour of depression, but most certainly one positive thing is the renewed and increased ability to enjoy, and no longer take for granted, simple everyday pleasures of life.

It seems to me that there must be a positive and a negative side to all aspects of life: there cannot be happiness without sorrow, light without darkness, goodness without evil, pleasure without pain, or life without death. Obviously, we have to seek the positive, and I think this can only be done by encountering the negative and overcoming it.

After I had experienced depression, I felt that it had been for me a necessary, if unwelcome part of life's teaching. We sometimes feel too sure of ourselves; too certain that we can control our own destiny. In depression that control is lost, and it is in acknowledging that we need more than our own resources, that we are able to find a power hidden deep within ourselves, the existence of which we had been formerly unaware. If our lives were always running on an even keel, we might never make that discovery. An old Persian poem expresses this very thought:-

> Be not thou as a jar laden with water
> And the lip stone dry;

Or as a rider, swiftly borne afar,
Who never feels the horse beneath his thigh.

Those who have known the grey world of depression and have then discovered reality once more, will never again accept things at their face value. An African proverb says, "You cannot tie water in a lump". To a people who had never seen ice, this seemed merely to be stating the obvious. But you can easily tie up a lump of ice: the seemingly impossible CAN be done.

Despite all appearances to the contrary, despite the seeming lack of progress and the growing feelings of futility, there IS a way out of the darkness of depression, and purpose and meaning in it. Regardless of our conviction that we cannot go on, we must continue the struggle. And when we do find the strength to persevere, the way must always be forwards towards the unknown, never back in an attempt to recapture what has been lost. Each step we take forward brings us a little nearer to the welcoming light that is shining for us there, at the tunnel's end.

# 12   What is Agoraphobia?

Agoraphobia, a condition which can develop from depression, certainly causes loneliness. It is sometimes described as being a fear of open spaces, but a more correct definition would be a fear to leave the safety of one's home. Sufferers are, therefore, trapped indoors, lonely but unable to seek the company of others.

The phobia or fear which makes them afraid to venture out may be of enclosed, rather than open, spaces; crowded trains or buses, busy supermarkets, or indeed any shops. Some agoraphobics fear traffic, and crossing the road becomes a formidable task, others find it impossible to visit the hairdresser; the thought of being trapped under the drier and unable to escape from the shop, fills them with terror.

Fear is one of the symptoms of depression, usually just a vague sense of foreboding; in agoraphobia it identifies itself with one particular activity, such as going into a busy shop. The agoraphobic person tries to ignore this feeling at first and continues to visit the supermarket. This causes the emotion of fear to intensify until it gets out of control and triggers off an attack of panic. Such attacks can be most distressing. The victim feels faint or breathless, the heartbeat may increase, or the sense of balance be lost. Fear becomes so extreme, that the natural instinct is to return as quickly as possible to the sanctuary of home. When the supermarket is entered the next time, the memory of that unpleasant attack returns and the pattern is repeated, so that eventually the agoraphobic person fears to leave home at all. Other phobias can develop in the same way, until the very possibility of venturing outside the front door seems unthinkable.

This build-up is caused by fear linked with panic, and once established is not easy to cure. However, much can be done to ease the condition, and most of the treatment suggested for depression applies equally here.

The term agoraphobic sounds so ominous that many sufferers consider themselves to be freaks and strive to keep their affliction a secret. Yet nearly everyone has a phobia of one sort or another, and to a greater or lesser degree. Most of us have a slight fear of something, be it spiders, snakes, mice, thunderstorms, heights, wasps, dark woods, churchyards, being alone in the house at night, and so on. But it is when that fear or revulsion at the thought of one of these becomes magnified into a state of terror and dread, that it can be classified as a phobia. Of all phobias, agoraphobia is probably the most common.

It is, of course, so easy for fear to develop and grow. A snowball rolling down a steep hill gathers more and more snow on the way. So, once fear is established, it will feed upon itself until it becomes unmanageable. The degree of fear is far greater than the situation justifies. Thus most people fail to understand why an agoraphobic sufferer looks in horror at the crowded shop, and finds it impossible to enter.

# 13 The Way to a Cure

## Acceptance

The first step is to accept the condition, recognise what it is, and above all, not to feel ashamed of it. It does not signify a weakness of character, nor is it a symptom of senility or madness. It is an illness which can be cured: no more and no less. We cannot ignore it, and it will not go away if we pretend it is not there. Nevertheless, acceptance is not the same as surrender, and we do not have to allow the agoraphobia to take control of us.

When we have 'flu', for instance, we accept that we are unwell and do not carry on with our work as usual. But neither do we sit in a chair and do nothing. We take the positive actions of getting any necessary medicine, staying in bed and keeping warm. By doing these things we are fighting the 'flu' virus and helping our bodies to recover in the shortest possible time. Similarly, in agoraphobia, although the treatment is different, we have to take positive steps to overcome it. For a while we must accept our limitations, relying, perhaps, on others to do the shopping, missing out on visits to friends and relations, and confining our exercise to work in the house and garden.

Sadly, it is not a condition which invites sympathy from others; they are more likely to react with impatience, and consider that it can be thrown off at will. We have to make up our minds, then, to recover by our own efforts and determination. It will take time and may be a slow process, but the rewards are great, and however hard it appears, it is not an impossible goal once we know how to set about achieving it.

## Relaxation

Fear produces tension in the body, and the agoraphobic live in a state of constant fear and anxiety. It is necessary to learn how to relax, and there are various ways in which this can be done. To succeed, daily practice is necessary until the body has been trained to release that accumulated tension and take life's pressures more calmly.

Set aside a short period each day for relaxation. Sit or lie comfortably. Try to empty your mind of worrying thoughts by concentrating on a beautiful picture, listening to soothing music, or imagining a peaceful scene such as a moonlit lake, a field of corn, or a snow-capped mountain. Then, very slowly, starting from the top of your head, deliberately tense up and then allow to relax each part of your body, until you are feeling really calm and rested. Breathe deeply and quietly. Let yourself become limp and heavy as though sinking down into the depths of a soft and billowing cloud.

There are some excellent cassettes on the market at present which will take you through this procedure, and it is often easier to follow instructions on a tape, rather than carrying out the routine by oneself.

When we have been under stress for a long period, it is not easy to be able to unwind. We may be desperately tired and yet unable to sleep. We may go on holiday and instead of finding relaxation we remain restless and full of tension. It is even possible to lie on a beach and yet feel rigid with anxiety; we may achieve a sun tan, but not a rested mind and body. The reason is that it is very difficult indeed to slow down and relax the sub-conscious mind. We try very hard to rest and unwind, but below the surface subconscious thoughts still churn in a turmoil. Deep, rather than superficial, relaxation is what we need to aim for. Meditation, once taught by the church, today more often in lay groups, is an excellent way of stilling the mind and bringing about inward peace.

My own remedy, and one which I can certainly recommend, is something I call 'crow's nesting'. When I was a child, my mother who was a keen gardener, could often be found at the end of the day sitting at the bedroom window and gazing into the garden, just enjoying its beauty. My father, who had been in the Navy, called that window 'the crow's nest', because this was the name of the look-out post at the top of the mast where sailors would sit to keep watch at sea. I used to enjoy looking out of our 'crow's nest' myself. I would fix my eyes on a flowering shrub or a patch of bright flowers, and allow my thoughts to wander. Somehow, worrying thoughts never intruded then, as they would have done if I had just been sitting in a chair and looking at nothing in particular, or if I had been lying in bed unable to sleep. The secret seems to be to fix one's eyes and thoughts on something beautiful; moving clouds, perhaps, on a summer's day, and then to let one's mind wander as it will.

River fishing is another way of relaxing. I prefer not to do it myself, because I do not particularly like the idea of catching the fish, but the therapy is in being alone with the moving water and gently swaying trees; occupied, and yet not under stress, almost, in fact, becoming at one with the living world around. We have to merge ourselves into our surroundings until the stress eases away, just as a fallow field is allowed to rest while the sunshine and air renew it. Some people can lose themselves in music, another good antidote to stress, or in prayer, when we can rest our burdens on God. I have always found comfort in these lines:-

Drop thy still dews of quietness,
Till all our strivings cease.

Take from our souls the strain and stress
And let our ordered lives confess
The beauty of Thy peace.


## How to cope with a panic attack

During a country walk, on a recent holiday, we came across a sheep which had somehow, in the curious manner that sheep have of getting themselves into awkward situations, become seprated from the rest of the flock. It wanted to rejoin them, but was prevented by a wire fence. On our approach it was thrown into a panic and began hurling itself in a frenzy against the wire to try to break through. We had to stop and wait for it to calm down, and then attempt to encourage it to move gently along the fence to the opening at the other end. We were able to see the way out, though the sheep could not. Our panic attacks are just the same. They serve only to make the situation worse, but we seem powerless to prevent them from occuring. What can be done?

Panic can be dealt with, though it is not easy. Think of it as a very large wave rolling in from the sea. Instead of letting it sweep us under, we have to get on top of it and ride in with it. We cannot stop it, but we can be in control of it.

When that first sensation of rising fear comes, STOP. Do not try to continue with what you were intending to do. Take six long, slow deep breaths. This always has a calming effect. Do not pretend that the difficulty is not there, or that there is no problem. That would be like telling the wave to stop moving. King Canute found how impossible THAT was! Instead, think "Well, I have a problem, but if I face it calmly and work through it a little at a time, I shall overcome it". Never push yourself too hard. If you are afraid of something, do not go at it head on. On the other hand, don't run away from it. Just work at it slowly, trying to get the better of it bit by bit. The proverb, 'softly, softly, catchee monkey', is a true one.

Panic, we must remember, will only make things worse, and the state of panic is what is most harmful. The sheep dashing itself against the wire was only risking injury, and not in the least helping its predicament. A fly caught in a cobweb will struggle, and only succeed in entangling itself the more; were it to attempt to bite away the restricting threads one at a time, it would stand a far better chance of escaping. We may find ourselves in dangerous situations where we need to act quickly. Here again panic is useless. If, in an accident, we must free a seat belt, or open a door or window, swift action does depend on a clear mind. Panic causes our fingers to fumble and our thinking to slow down. It is never anything but destructive.

Sometimes, in an attack, it helps if we can focus on something that will distract our minds from the situation causing distress; saying the alphabet backwards, for example, or sipping a glass of water slowly. I have a friend who suffers from breathless attacks, and have found that the best way to get her over one of these is to tell her a joke or amusing story. By thinking of this she is able to forget momentarily the frightening circumstances which had upset her, and once the first sensation of panic is over, she is able to cope once more.

## Steps to Recovery

Recovery is always easier if we have a sympathetic friend or relative who is able to assist us. Agoraphobics can often face leaving their homes if someone is with them. However, even if the battle has to be fought alone, it can still be won. The secret is to be content to take one step at a time, and to record all progress. This recording is most important for it will encourage us, and when we look back through the pages we will be able to assess how much improvement has been made. Of course, we shall fail sometimes; often, in fact, but failures are never to be recorded. We have to train ourselves to disregard them; they do not matter, and have no place in our progress record.

The first thing is to plan ahead for the next day. Devise some small step. It may only be to open the front door and peep outside. If you did not want to do it, it was an achievement. It can now be recorded as that day's success. On the following day, aim at walking to the front gate, and so on. If a panic attack comes, do not worry. Stop, breathe deeply, and allow it to pass. Do not force yourself to go on. Return home and try again the next day. And don't worry about it. It is bound to happen, but these attacks will lessen as your confidence is built up.

It often helps to give some small reward if you cope with a difficult situation. Be kind to yourself. Promise yourself a little treat each time you gain any set target. More encouragement is available if you are in touch with other sufferers. The Open Door Association will help you to make contacts, and can offer additional advice.

The important thing is never to feel that you are beyond help, or that you have been agoraphobic for so long that nothing can be done in your case. If you want to be well, you will be; the dreadful loneliness of agoraphobia CAN be overcome. There is always a way out.

# Positive and Negative Actions

## For Depression

DO    seek medical help.

DO    accept your depression. Neither fear it nor be ashamed of it.

DO    make up your mind that you will overcome it, steadily and patiently, one step at a time.

DO    go out as much as possible and take some form of exercise.

DO    eat sensibly and regularly.

DO    learn to do and think positively.

DO    learn how to relax.

DO    make contacts with others who will understand and help you.
and most important of all, NEVER GIVE UP HOPE.

DON'T    think you are all alone in the world. Others do care.

DON'T    feel a freak. Depression is a common condition.

DON'T    rely on props like cigarettes or alcohol; they increase rather than lessen depression.

DON'T    feel a failure or useless.

DON'T    give up; suicide is never the answer.

## For Agoraphobia

DO    accept it.

DO    determine that you will overcome it.

| | |
|---|---|
| Do | learn how to relax. |
| Do | make haste slowly. |
| Do | record your successes. |
| Do | give yourself small rewards |
| Don't | be afraid of fear. Panic attacks always pass. |
| Don't | record or remember failures. |
| Don't | believe that you cannot be cured. |

# Part III
# Learning to Live Alone

# 14  A House or a Home

Home: I suppose no other word in our language can hold such a wealth of meaning. It is so much more than just a place where we eat, sleep and find shelter. For those who live alone it is very important that the place where they live is indeed a home to them, a refuge from stresses and strains.

All houses have an atmosphere of their own which is apparent as soon as you enter them. I have been into houses which welcomed me, and into others where I was uncomfortable and ill at ease, though being on equally friendly terms with the respective owners. I once stayed in a house which was reputed to be haunted by the previous occupier who had built it and loved it all his life. I'm not sure if I believe in conventional ghosts, but I always had a fondness for that house myself, and when alone there, although it was an old rambling place full of mysterious noises and dark corners, I never felt at all nervous. The house itself seemed friendly and protective as if my 'ghost', though regretful to leave, was approving of my presence there. Both this house and a small country cottage in which I lived some years later used to give me the impression, as I came back to them at the end of the day, that they were glad to welcome me home.

Most of us have experienced being in a room which has been furnished and decorated in such a way as to set our teeth on edge. Everyone's taste is so different, and of course this is a very good thing. Life would be dull indeed if we all lived in identical little compartments. The important thing is that the rooms we live in should feel right to us. We should be in harmony with the things which surround us. I can remember how much I hated my grandparents' front parlour. I can see now the dark, heavy furniture with its black leather upholstery, the dreary patterned wallpaper, and the venetian blinds always kept half-closed to protect the carpet from sunlight. Truly, a room to chill the stoutest heart.

If you live alone the first thing to do is to ensure that you live not just in a house, but in a home. It may be that being alone has been suddenly thrust upon you by bereavement, or by children leaving home. You may have had to move to a new town in order to obtain work, or you may be just setting out at the start of your adult life to live in a room or flat of your own. Whatever the circumstances, it is up to you to create a home for yourself in which you will feel happy and contented.

Take a careful look at the room in which you are now sitting. Does it really please you? As your eyes travel round it, do you feel sensations of pleasure and contentment as you consider each item of furniture and ornament? It may be that the room is nothing more to you than a convenient place in which to eat and rest; and yet the greatest asset of living alone is that you are free to make the most of your environment, adapting it to the way of life which you find most convenient and most satisfying. Many things can be done, with little or no expense, to give a house the character of a home. We will consider them in turn.

## Light

Nothing is more depressing than a room which faces north and gets little direct sunlight, or from which the light is blocked by overhanging trees or neighbouring high buildings. Unless you live in only one room, this can easily be remedied by making the dark room into your bedroom and simply transferring the furniture. If this means that you must live upstairs and sleep on the ground floor, why should it be a problem? There is no logical reason for having to go upstairs to bed. Those who live in flats or bungalows find no difficulty in living on one level. In fact, the novelty of a change of rooms can be quite stimulating.

Do not despair though if you live in a single gloomy room. Much can be done to improve it. If you can buy new furniture opt for light rather than dark wood. White doors and white paint work reflect light, and wall mirrors brighten a room. Careful curtain choice will give windows a cheerful look, and if the view outside is dreary, shut it out by using crisp nets in addition to the main curtains. Loose covers for the armchairs, colourful cushions, pictures, ornaments, plants, screens, and rugs will all help to give character to your room and make it a pleasure to live in.

## Colour

Colour can influence us more than perhaps we realise, and even change our mood. The combination of colours in house decoration can sometimes be aesthetically charming or in other cases absolutely disastrous, so we have to be very careful to choose a colour scheme that is right for us. Some basic factors have first to be considered. Blue, grey, green and mauve are cool colours and should be avoided in cold dark rooms, while orange, yellow and gold give a feeling of warmth. Bright reds and purples are hard colours and too much of them in a room can be overpowering. Brown, beige and grey will combine well with other shades, but if chosen as the predominant colour the effect will be sombre. Cream or magnolia walls have a softer appearance than plain white. The main consideration is to look for colours which are pleasing to you. To one person a yellow painted room can give the effect of sunshine, while to another it suggests jaundice; coloured ceilings may inspire some, while others will find them oppressive. The choice is yours and the right colour scheme can transform a room. If it pleases you then you have made the right choice.

## Furnishings

Comfort and convenience should be the main objectives. It is vital to have at least one really comfortable chair that is the right height for you, so that you can relax in it without feeling cramped, or finding that when you lean back your feet will not touch the floor. A footstool is sometimes a helpful addition. An uncluttered room makes housework very much easier. It is well worth selling unnecessary or cumbersome items of furniture that overcrowd your living space. On the other hand you must have adequate cupboards or shelving so that odds and ends can be tidily stored away, and you will need enough chairs for visiting relatives or friends. If you are dissatisfied with the appearance of your armchairs or settee it is surprising what a difference loose covers can make. A comfortable bed is important too. A sagging and lumpy mattress can seriously affect your sleeping and general health.

## Smaller Furniture

It is the smaller items which give individuality to a home. Never choose a picture because it is fashionable; only if you are really attracted to it. Remember that it will be your constant companion, year in and year out, and you must be able to live with it. Because of this it is sometimes worth saving to buy an original painting if it seems beautiful to you, rather than opting for a cheaper but indifferent print. However, price is not always a true guide in the world of art. Best of all, of course, if you have any artistic talent, or even if you don't, is to paint your own picture!

Ornaments too should only find houseroom if they are

dearly loved, either for their own intrinsic beauty, or as souvenirs of past happy events. Family photographs will surround you with memories and bring friends and relatives closer, but do not display them if they evoke regret for the past and make you feel sad.

Doubtless you will have a television and a radio, and if you like music a record player or a cassette recorder is a useful friend. We must look at the clock a hundred times a day, so be sure to have one with a shape and face that pleases you and whose tick is companionable rather than obstrusive.

## Warmth

The focal point of most living rooms is the fire, and whether it is coal, gas, electric, or a solid fuel stove, it must look both welcoming and cheerful. Warmth in winter is essential. There is nothing more depressing than a bleak, chilly room. See that doors and windows are draught-proofed. A door curtain or draught excluder will add comfort, and so will a thick hearthrug. If your room is heated by warm air or storage heaters it is still possible to make a focal point either of the television or by using a mock fireplace.

## Further Considerations

Re-arranging furniture can make quite a difference to the appearance of a room. Sometimes dividing it into two separate areas can change its character and add interest. Good lighting is essential, especially if you do much reading or close work, and wall or table lamps often give a more pleasing effect than a central fitting. There is a wide choice of lampshades, and these too can indicate your special interests. I love wild flowers and was delighted when I found two lamps with pressed flowers incorporated into the shades, so that they seem to come to life when the light is switched on.

Do not be afraid to experiment or to display the things that please you. Teenagers, being less inhibited than their elders, often festoon their rooms with cut-outs of favourite pop stars, or hang them about with posters and mobiles. The Victorians, who loved their homes, used to decorate screens with postcards and embroider their own samplers and covers. Why should we not do likewise? Things which you make yourself will give you pleasure to create and will undoubtedly add charm and individuality to your home.

# 15  Pets, Plants and Paraphernalia

Having considered the main furnishings of your home we can now turn to the optional, but all-important, extras.

> "Oh I wish, how I wish
> That I had a little house,
> With a cat for the mat,
> And a holey for the mouse....."

went the Nursery song, and indeed for many people a home without a cat or a dog would be incomplete. Many doctors believe that caring for an animal is beneficial, particularly for people on their own. An animal provides company, and because dogs need exercise, their owners also benefit from the daily walk. The need to buy and prepare food for a pet will sometimes stimulate elderly people to buy food for themselves at the same time. They are often more aware of their pets' needs than their own.

In addition to this, contact with living creatures, and particularly stroking them, has a therapeutic value and a soothing effect on the nerves. Dentists have discovered that a tank of fish in the waiting room will calm apprehensive patients, so if you are unable to keep more active pets it might be worth considering whether fish or birds would appeal to you. A friend of mine has an African grey parrot of great character and with a choice turn of language! Her friends find it very entertaining. Sometimes pets can themselves be a means of making new friends, as many guide dog owners have found. People will come up to admire the animal and in doing so will start a conversation with its owner. Dogs obviously provide protection for those who live alone, and will give early warning of anyone approaching the door. Even the most docile and friendly of dogs will deter a potential burglar by its mere presence, because he has no way of knowing how it would react were he to try to force an entrance.

However, not everyone feels the need to have a pet, and problems can arise if you wish to go on holiday. In many flats the keeping of cats or dogs is forbidden, and in this sort of housing, with no easy access to a garden, it would in any case be unsuitable for most animals. It is still possible, though, to care for living things in the form of plants and flowers.

If your house has a garden and if you enjoy gardening you have a very healthy hobby which can bring considerable pleasure and satisfaction. Being in contact with growing things is a great reliever of stress and tension. A garden gives the opportunity to grow your own fruit and vegetables which, as well as costing so much less than those bought in the supermarket, will also be much fresher and more appetising. You have the opportunity, if you wish, to make your own jam, bottled fruit and chutney, and to freeze vegetables for winter use. A garden is a very peaceful place, giving you your own private sanctuary. On a hot summer's day what could be more restful than to sit on the grass under a shady tree and watch the busy traffic of butterflies and bees among the flowers? Flowers are very expensive to buy, but when you are able to grow your own you can enjoy them in abundance.

Flat dwellers or the elderly, for whom gardening is no longer possible, do not have to live without plants. Houseplants are now available in more varieties than ever before, and some are very hardy and easy to care for. Most are supplied with full instructions as to watering and the sort of conditions which they prefer. Although some require more water than others, the golden rule is usually not to over-water. Plants can add much to the character of a room, and we have come a long way from Victorian times when a stiff aspidistra was almost the only houseplant known. Herbs, such as parsley, mustard and cress can be grown in the kitchen and picked as required. Special growing pots are on sale, but mustard and cress can just as easily germinate in a saucer on damp lint or blotting paper. Some people enjoy growing cacti of which there is a wonderful variety. In fact, the growing of indoor plants can become so fascinating that we have to beware of their taking over the room and turning it into a green jungle!

I have included under the heading 'paraphernalia' collections of all kinds, including books. Not everyone enjoys reading, but for those who do, the provision of books will be a very necessary part of the furnishing of their home.

> Give a man a pipe he can smoke,
> Give a man a book he can read:
> And his home is bright with a calm delight,
> Though the room be poor indeed.     *J. Thomson*

Books open so many doors and satisfy so many moods and requirements. We use them for relaxation, for reference, for escape, to cheer us up, to help us to understand more about the world we live in, or for sheer pleasure. If you are a real book lover you will certainly have many that are old friends and that you have read over and over again. Books to pass an idle hour or to help to relieve the monotony of a long journey might well be a paperback or a loan from the library, but a shelf or bookcase full of well-loved volumes is an essential part of a home. Holiday guides, street maps and even school atlases will possibly form part of such a collection that has built up over the years, and the variety of books will reveal the tastes and preferences of their owner.

Not everyone is a collector, even of books, but nowadays more and more people are finding the attraction of building up sets of interesting objects. They may be china bells, pottery animals, sea shells, stamps, postcards, decorative boxes, antique spoons, pressed flowers—in fact almost anything. If you have this sort of hobby then you will want to display your collection so that it can be seen to its best advantage. Try to make it a feature of the room so that you are able to enjoy it fully.

If, when you look round your room, you see other items not mentioned so far but which you feel are necessary for you to have, then this is all to the good. Your home should express your personality, and the more originality it contains the more likely it will be to suit your own particular requirements. It doesn't matter in the least if some of the furniture is a bit shabby; there is no need to have every cushion and cover in perfect order; it doesn't matter how large or how small it is, or whether the curtains are luxury velvet or of cheapest gingham. What does matter is that it should convey to you feelings of comfort and security and, above all, of home.

# 16   Cooking for One

Catering for one person is full of pitfalls. It is so easy to be tempted to make do with something which will not involve much preparation or washing up. The danger is that too much dependence on convenience foods may, while satisfying hunger, add up to a very unbalanced diet, which will result in poor health and a lowered resistance to disease. Buying food in sufficiently small quantities can also present problems, for it is more satisfactory to cook only as much as will be required at any one time. Left-over food which is later re-heated loses some of its nourishment and may carry a risk of food poisoning. In any case it is boring to repeat the same meal on consecutive days. Food should be enjoyed, and cooking it a pleasant experience. It is important to observe a healthy and nutritious diet, and daily rations should include at least one item from each of the following categories:-

1.   Meat, fish, cheese or eggs.
2.   Some fruit, and some vegetables.
3.   Bread, or other grain product.
4.   Some milk, and some butter or margarine.

Fibrous foods should be added, because these help to keep us healthy. They are bran, oatmeal, wholemeal bread, and raw vegetables or fruit. Sugar and all sweet foods; jam, cakes, biscuits and chocolate, are pleasant extras but non-essentials. Indeed, too much sugar can be harmful. It is also beneficial to drink plenty of fluid; tea, coffee, fruit juice, or just plain water.

The frying pan should be utilised only sparingly. While fried food is tasty and easily prepared, it can also be indigestible, and a diet over-rich in fat is certainly detrimental to health. Grilling is a better alternative. A small casserole is invaluable for the person living alone. Food prepared in this will not dry up, and the natural juices are preserved. There is an added advantage in that the oven stays cleaner when a covered, greased casserole is used.

Should cooking present problems, the doctor or social worker would be able to arrange for the 'Meals on Wheels' service to supply a hot dinner daily. Many towns have luncheon clubs for the elderly, where cheap but nourishing meals may be obtained.

The following hints may also help in making the best and most economical use of food supplies:-

**Bread** New bread can be cut more easily by using a knife that has been dipped in boiling water.
Dip a stale loaf in cold water and heat it in the oven until it is dry. Then wrap in a damp cloth and cool.

**Cakes** If a cake sticks to the tin, stand it for a few minutes on a damp cloth while it is still hot.

**Cheese** Grated cheese goes further and keeps longer.

**Eggs** If you are going to boil an egg, prick it first with a pin and the shell is less likely to crack in the pan.
Eggs can be separated by inverting an eggcup gently over the yolk and then straining off the white.
Wrap a cracked egg tightly in foil before boiling. This will prevent the white from escaping.

**Foil** A small joint sometimes gets very dry and shrinks during cooking. If wrapped in foil, it will stay moister and the oven will need less cleaning. Wrap the foil loosely, but secure the edges well.

**Jam** If an opened jar of jam or honey goes hard and sugary, stand it in a saucepan of water and heat it gently.

**Milk** When heating milk, rinse the pan with cold water first. It is then less likely to stick. A marble in the pan will stop it from boiling over.

**Onions** If they are peeled under water your eyes will not be affected.

**Pastry** For light pastry, cool the fat in the refrigerator, then shred it with a coarse grater before rubbing into the flour.

**Potatoes** Baked potatoes in jackets will cook quicker if a skewer is pushed through.
A wire pan-scourer is useful for scraping new potatoes. It removes only a thin layer of skin, leaving behind the vitamins which are stored just below it.

**Prunes** Soak prunes overnight in cold tea and cook them in the same liquid. This gives them a delicious flavour.

**Tomatoes** Immerse in boiling water for a few seconds before removing the skins. They will then peel easily.

**Vegetables** Whenever possible, make use of water in which vegetables have been boiled as it contains much of their goodness.
When draining cooked vegetables, turn on the cold tap as this will cut down the amount of steam in the kitchen.

# 17   Looking After Yourself

It is well worth taking precautions in order to obtain peace of mind when living alone. If your front door is secured by a chain which will only allow it to be partially opened, no caller can enter except at your invitation. Those who come on official business from the Council, the electricity or gas boards, or similar bodies, will always carry identification cards, and you should ask to see their credentials before you invite them in. A spy hole in a door will also enable you to check on visitors before opening to them. The back door should have a secure lock and bolt, and if you live on the ground floor, or in a vulnerable place, it is worth considering having window locks fitted also. Ladders should never be left where a burglar can take advantage of them, and if you go out in the evening a room light left burning will give the impression that the house is still occupied.

Another hazard of living alone is locking yourself out. It is not a good idea to hide a spare key under a flower pot or on a string inside the letter box. A would-be burglar could so easily discover it. It is wiser to leave a key with a trustworthy neighbour or friend, or to carry an extra one on a ring and secured by a safety pin (preferably the type with a self-locking head) to the inside of your coat pocket.

A telephone should be considered as a necessity rather than a luxury. It is so much more convenient, if you are suddenly taken ill, to be able to phone the doctor from the warmth of your own home. In the event of an emergency it could even be a life-saver. As well as this, it provides an immediate way of contacting friends for a chat, and incoming calls add interest and variety to the day.

## Self-sufficiency

It is advisable to be prepared for any emergencies. A small store of candles, fixed securely into jars, a torch and a box of matches, can be kept in a handy place in readiness for any power cuts or electrical failure. Do you know where to turn off the gas, electricity or water supply should the need arise?

It is helpful to keep spare electric light bulbs, replacement fuses and fuse wire, tap washers and so on with basic tools for small repair jobs such as a hammer, screwdriver, small nails and screws, pliers and lubricating oil. You may be skilled at home maintenance, in which case your tool kit would need to be much more extensive, and if you enjoy doing your own painting and decorating you will doubtless already have a supply of equipment for this. For jobs you are unable to tackle on your own, keep the phone number of your plumber, electrician and carpenter, together with those of the doctor, dentist and taxi rank near to the telephone, so that you will not need to waste time in searching for them in a case of urgency.

When changing a fuse yourself, remember to turn off at the mains first. If a light or mains fuse blows you will have to find the faulty one in the main fuse box and re-wire it. A fuse in most electrical appliances has to be replaced in the plug. In this case, first switch off both the appliance itself and the plug, then replace the dead fuse with a new one, making sure that it is the correct amp. number.

Wiring a plug is not too difficult providing you remember the appropriate colours; blue for neutral, green or yellow for earth, and brown for live. An easy way to remember which wire to attach to each terminal is to hold the plug upright with the pins pointing away from you.

The wire which goes to the left terminal is blue; *l* for left and the second letter of b*l*ue. The wire which goes to the right terminal is brown; *r* for right and the second letter of b*r*own. The flex goes into the bottom of the plug after you have stripped back about 2 inches of the outer sheath to reveal the three coloured wires.

## Safety Precautions

Chip pans are the most common cause of kitchen fires; never leave the pan unattended.

Cover frying pans with a splatter guard.

Keep a fire-smothering cloth in a handy position in the kitchen.

Turn all saucepan handles inwards.

Do not dry tea towels over a naked gas flame.

Do not fix a mirror over the fireplace. There is a risk of clothing touching the fire when you go near it.

Keep inflammable liquids and aerosols away from any source of heat.

Unplug all electrical points at night and shut inner doors.

It is safer to stand on a step-stool with a guard bar at the top when changing a light bulb than to balance on a chair.

Wet floors are slippery.

Loose mats can be dangerous and floors under mats should not be polished. A rubber mat reduces the risk of slipping in the bath, and the elderly should consider having a bath rail fitted for added security.

It is unwise to switch off hall and stair lights to economise on electricity. The amount of money saved is negligible and dark areas can be dangerous.

## First Aid

Always keep a small first-aid kit (bandages, lint, sticking plaster, scissors, tweezers, antiseptic, anti-histamine cream and aspirins) in a convenient place. Many people have this in the bathroom, but the kitchen is often the place where cuts and burns occur, so it is wise to have some sticking plaster at least in one of the kitchen drawers.

A burn is eased by holding it under the cold tap. Ice is good for bumps and bruises. Wrap first in a paper tissue and then hold over the affected area.

## Warmth

Warmth is very necessary for well being, and hypothermia is a winter hazard, particularly in the elderly who are unable to keep as active as the young. Thermal underwear and woollen clothing will help, and so will electric blankets, but it is best to buy only those with a BEAB mark or label which guarantees safety. Remember too that they should be serviced at least once every three years.

If the winter is severe and the house has no central heating, it may be healthier to sleep in the warmest room rather than in an unheated bedroom.

## Money Matters

For safety's sake never keep in the house more cash than you require for immediate needs. A bank, the post office or a building society will not only guard your money securely, but will provide you with interest on it. It is not really a good idea to buy television, electricity or gas stamps. You have to purchase them before the bill is due, and use money which could be making you interest. Also, if you lose them you have no way of reclaiming the loss. It is better to keep the money in the bank and write down in a notebook the amounts which you need to set aside to meet the different bills.

Check that both your house itself and the contents (your furniture and personal possessions) are adequately insured. Many people underestimate the value of their house contents. It is worth while spending a little time in working out what it would cost to replace them should you be unfortunate enough to have a serious fire. Insurances should be index-linked, so that even in times of inflation the correct cover is maintained.

## Holidays

Last, but not least, remember that a good holiday is a very necessary part of looking after yourself. A break away from everyday surroundings and a change in the pattern of your day is very beneficial to health, and however enjoyable the holiday, you will appreciate the familiarity of your home the more when you return.

# 18   Making Friends

On the whole, those who are happiest living alone are people who would normally expect to spend a full day in the company of others, and then look forward to a quiet and relaxed evening following their own inclinations without anything to distract them. This, of course, presupposes that they already have friends and companions. Sadly, there are many who, for one reason or another, find that there is no one they could really count as a friend. Many elderly couples have moved to a new area on retirement. They have been happy in each other's company and have not troubled to look for outside interests. Then, when one dies, the other is left with no one to turn to. There are also the very shy and withdrawn folk who are never comfortable in pubs or clubs, who feel awkward at dances or discos, and although they long to make friends, simply do not know how to set about it. Single, divorced or separated people frequently find that married couples do not seem to welcome their company, and those who are trying to bring up children in a one-parent family are so tied by their home responsibilities that there is little time for making contacts with others. This is when loneliness sets in, and people feel trapped and shut into themselves. Even worse is the plight of the agoraphobics, whose fears imprison them in their own homes.

The problem is to know how to set about making friends. Friendship is rather like happiness. If you try too hard to find it, it will elude you; if you turn your back on it, it will often creep up on you unawares. People who are desperate for friendship can easily drive potential friends away by being too persistent and clinging. True friendship can only grow naturally. It cannot be earned, or bought, or given as an obligation.

I think the first thing to do is merely to put yourself where you will be in the company of others. Shopping, waiting at a bus stop, going on a coach trip, attending church, visiting a club or joining an evening class will all achieve this. Even then, it is perfectly possible to come and go without saying a word to anyone, so a further effort has to be made. Look for someone else who is alone, rather than trying to break into a group, and make a casual remark. How useful is the weather on such occasions! If the person you speak to is willing to follow it up, all well and good, but if not, then try someone else. But never rush things, or attach yourself firmly to someone unless they too show that they are willing to carry on with the conversation. Don't expect too much. Be content at first just with companionship rather than friendship, and try to have a few words with as many people as you can during the course of each day. Make a point of passing a remark to the girl at the check-out in the supermarket, the postman, the milkman and so on, and soon you will find it easier to make contacts with others.

Some people find conversation difficult. This need not be a barrier. A good listener is much more likely to be popular than someone who never stops talking. Just be interested in those you meet and let them do the talking. It is easier to chat to those with whom you share a common interest, so if you are enthusiastic about dogs, bingo, gardening, antiques, music or whatever else takes your fancy, try to find a club, or association, or charity which focuses on this and go along to take part or to offer help. Your library will have a list of all clubs and organisations in the area. In this way you will meet people who are 'on your wavelength', and you will find them easier to talk to.

Best of all are the pastimes in which you have to take an active part yourself. Any type of sport, amateur dramatics or singing in a choir would come into this category, and would certainly involve you in others' company.

If, however, you still have difficulty in relating to those around you, the best thing to do is to seek out groups of people who would welcome you for what you are able to give to them. You will feel more at ease with those who are looking to you for help. If you like children some Play Groups, Nursery and Infants' schools are glad of assistance. Hospitals and Old People's Homes provide opportunities for visiting, and libraries are often grateful for volunteers to take books to the housebound. Perhaps you could give someone in a wheelchair an outing, or try your hand at baby (or granny)-sitting. A small advertisement in a local paper or shop offering your services in this way will usually bring a response. Contacts made like this can easily build up into friendships. Charity shops are another possibility. By working in one of these you will meet people all day long.

The important thing is to make a start, no matter in how small a way, to widen your circle and your interests so that you have as many opportunities as you can of being involved with others. If all else fails, try finding a pen friend; exchanging letters can be very rewarding.

But if, despite all your efforts, you are still lonely, do not be afraid to ask for help. A ship in trouble sends out an S.O.S. If it did not, it would go on drifting into danger, while the coastguards, lifeboat men, and helicopter crews who would have been ready to help, would be ignorant of its plight. Who will help you? There are quite a number of sources, depending on your age, circumstances, and needs; but your doctor, vicar, social service, and voluntary services are just a few. Then there are the associations for helping the elderly, one-parent families, widows and widowers. Contact and Age Concern are both particularly anxious to combat loneliness in the elderly. Your local library will have a record of all the social and self-help groups in your area. Finally, there are other lonely people who would be only too glad to make new friends.

# 19   The Need to be Occupied

The camel's hump is an ugly lump
As well you may see at the Zoo,
But uglier yet is the hump we get
From having too little to do *(Kipling)*

When we live in the company of others there are constant demands on our time. Things are happening all around us, and we become involved in the doings of others throughout the day. A person living alone, however, can all too easily find time hanging heavily, with an expanse of the day stretching ahead, empty and uninviting. To be happy and contented it is essential to be fully occupied; times of rest and relaxation are necessary, but only as interludes between satisfying activities,

The problem is not so great for those who are in fulltime employment, returning home to spend the evening alone. After a tiring day associating with fellow workers, a quiet evening can offer real enjoyment; or there is the choice of going out with friends or asking them round for a meal. Loneliness is much more likely to strike the retired person, or those who, for one reason or another, have to spend most of the day at home. It is most necessary for these people to plan for themselves a daily programme of interesting activities.

Far from regretting the cessation of continuous employment, retired people should rejoice in the freedom which they now possess and use it to the full, not to fritter away the idle hours, but to fill them with new pleasures. Now there is no need to watch the clock, to cope with tedious office business, to travel in discomfort during the rush hour, or to spend the best hours of a summer's day shut in a stuffy room. Now is the time to take up new hobbies, new sports, voluntary activities, club memberships, to learn new crafts or languages, to go on coach trips and excursions and so on; the list is endless. A golden rule is always, if you are in good health, to go out for at least part of every day. It may only be a visit to the local shops, but it takes you into the company of others and so breaks the monotony of a solitary existence.

The person who lives alone is at a considerable advantage when indulging in a chosen hobby or pastime. No one will object to the amount of time given to it or to any mess or noise involved. Some hobbies, indeed, can be enjoyed far better in solitude. Fishing needs quiet concentration with no distractions, and so does painting. Those who are interested in bird-watching can best carry out their observations alone, and of course, to listen to music or read a good book we do not need the company of others. Evening hours or brief periods during the day can usefully be filled with knitting, sewing, doing crossword puzzles (a very good mental exercise to keep the mind alert), jigsaws, scrabble or card games. There is a very good book in the *Teach Yourself* series called *Card Games for One* by George Hervey, which includes 87 variations of playing 'patience'.

I think it is a good thing for a retired person to decide on a new type of work on which to be occupied for the greater part of the day, with hobbies and other favourite pursuits in addition, to give variety. The new work, of course, will be chosen to provide pleasure rather than profit, but there is no reason why it should not also be financially rewarding if such employment is available. Many older people have attempted writing, and articles for local magazines are often in demand. Those who like gardening can sell their produce, or use it to make jam, pickles, chutney, bottled fruit, wine etc. Herbs, cut flowers, and bedding plants have a ready market also. In many places allotments are available for the physically active, and the services of an odd-job man, decorator, window cleaner, gardener, home help and other assistants are always required, even in days of recession. Charity shops need staff, and all charities welcome flag sellers. The local voluntary sevices are usually pleased to have extra help. The feeling of tiredness which comes at the end of a busy day spent in some worthwhile task, when achievements have been made, is very different from the lassitude which comes from boredom. There is great satisfaction in sinking into a chair in the evening and relaxing in front of the television, knowing that a good day's work is behind you. As the village blacksmith found, "something attempted, something done, has earned a night's repose".

There are some, however, who are unable to involve themselves in these active pursuits. The very elderly or infirm, or those who are confined to their homes by agoraphobia or crippling illness, must spend long hours alone within four walls. It is these people who are most prone to loneliness, and for whom being fully and gainfully occupied is the biggest problem. It is not an impossible one, though, and with careful thought and planning these folk too can spend their days happily. I have a blind friend who frequently cooks meals for her elderly neighbours. My friend's mother, now aged ninety, still sews and mends for other patients in the nursing home where she lives, most of them much younger than herself. There are many occupations for the housebound, and the wisest thing to do is to make a selection of these in order to provide an interesting programme throughout the day. Here are a few suggestions:-

Indoor gardening. Miniature gardens are fascinating, and so are collections of cacti. Herbs can be grown in the kitchen, and some plants, like African violets, can be propagated by taking cuttings. Window boxes too can be very colourful.

Bird watching. Birds can easily be attracted to a balcony or window sill by setting up a bird table, nesting boxes or a tit feeder. Coconuts and strings of nuts will quickly bring tits to your window.

Keep a diary.

Local leaders of Scout, Guide or Brownie groups are often glad of volunteers to test children in their homes for various badges.

Oxfam and other charities seek help in sorting stamps, coins or clothes.

Try a new skill. Learn to paint (even if only painting by numbers). Try writing a poem, story or article, or making up a crossword puzzle.

Sometimes Infant schools or playgroups need help in mending toys, books etc.

Make soft toys or knitted goods for bazaars or charities.

Take a correspondence course. Find out about ancient civilizations, learn another language, or if you are really ambitious get a degree with the Open University; there is no age limit.

Make a family scrapbook using old photographs, letters etc. Trace your family tree.

Make use of jigsaw puzzles, cards, scrabble etc.

Have a Coffee Morning in support of a charity and invite your neighbours in.

Always set aside part of each day to reading the newspaper carefully. To be well informed about what is happening in the world means that you are taking an active part yourself, and you can use your vote intelligently when the occasion arises to influence, in however small a way, the trends of events. It enables you to join in conversation with others about current affairs and to express opinions of your own.

For all who live alone some part of the day has to be given to housework and house care. Housework can be monotonous, but it helps to have a routine, doing specific jobs on each day, rather than leaving everything until the house is in such a mess that a mammoth cleaning operation becomes necessary. Many people clean one room thoroughly each day. However, any routine should be flexible, so that it can be discarded should the need arise. Another joy about living alone is that if you are halfway through cleaning the kitchen floor when you have an invitation to go out there is no harm at all in leaving everything in complete chaos to wait until you return. Rules are made to be broken! However, on the whole it is much easier to clean little and often. If, for instance, the cooker is given a quick wipe round after every use, cleaning it does not build up into a dirty and exhausting chore.

If you are active enough to do your own painting and decorating this is a great advantage. Not only does it save you considerable expense, but you are able to choose colours and quality of materials and know that the work has been properly carried out. Remember never to neglect painting the outside of your property, and watch window frames for signs of weathering. If you are thinking of installing double glazing it is worth noting that the type with UPVC frames does not require painting so that this, over the years, will be a saving.

Older people when shopping should not carry too much weight. Shopping trolleys will help to take the strain off your arms and back, but if you live within easy reach of shops a daily trip is advisable. This means that you will have less to carry and also the opportunity of meeting others and so adding variety to your day.

Being busy is certainly an antidote to loneliness. If you feel miserable get up and do something, even if it is only tidying a cupboard. And never sit down with a worry; if your mind has something else to occupy it, worrying thoughts have to be put to one side.

# 20   Loneliness or Solitude?

Loneliness is in the mind. Throughout the ages there have been men and women who have chosen to live a solitary life and have found joy in it. Hermits, prophets and seekers after truth have found that by living apart from their fellow men they have been able to come closer to understanding the mysteries of the Universe. Jesus himself, though being for most of His life in the closest possible contact with humanity, chose first to spend forty days of solitude in the wilderness. There are great benefits in being alone and one of these is that we are then able to use and develop our minds and our powers of thought and meditation. In these days of rush and noise and constant pressure the word 'meditation' sounds almost mediaeval and conjures up pictures of monks pacing the cloisters. But we are the losers if we neglect it.

We do need to form opinions on the great issues of our times; how to avert the threat of nuclear war, the problems of unemployment, inflation, and racism; whether we approve or not of space exploration, enthanasia, birth control, more permissive conduct between the sexes, and our views on politics and the existence or otherwise of God. It is not enough for our own ultimate satisfaction to take on at second hand the conclusions reached in a book or a newspaper, or those held by our parents or friends. We need to seek the answers in our own minds, and we can only do this if we can set aside a space of time for thought. Too many people when asked for an opinion can only swell the numbers of the uncommitted or 'Don't knows'.

I think it is sad that so frequently people are attended wherever they go by the constantly blaring noise from a transistor, so that they can never be alone with only their own thoughts for company. Indeed there are some who cannot bear silence even for a moment, and immediately on entering a room must turn on the radio or television. Stress is bound to build up if we continue to live at this pace. I remember once, when I was at the hairdresser's, I happened to be the last customer. As the assistant switched off the drier, the girl who was attending to my hair said, "For goodness sake turn it on again. I can't stand the awful quiet!"

Few of us though are hermits by nature. We need some social activity and companionship, the sound of other voices and perhaps also of music; but we need quiet periods in addition. To be truly happy and satisfied I think we need a mixture of all those ingredients and we should be able to find enough resources within ourselves to really enjoy and benefit from the hours of solitude.

Although many are unhappy at living alone, there are probably as many more who envy them and long for peace, quiet and independence. Some in overcrowded properties or in residential homes feel resricted and have little privacy. They have to endure closed windows and stuffy rooms, or open windows and draughts, over-loud television or programmes that bore them to fit in with the wishes of others, shared bedrooms, unappetising food, noise and cramped conditions. To have a home of their own with freedom to do as they please would, to their minds, be sheer bliss. So never feel deprived if you live alone, but set about learning the technique of living this sort of life. If, at the end of a visit from friends, you can bid them goodbye with no regrets and really look forward to enjoying the rest of the day in your own company, then you will have succeeded in doing so.

Recently I discovered some words which sum up very well all that I have been trying to convey:-

> Our language has wisely sensed the two sides of man's being alone. It has created the word loneliness to express the pain of being alone, and it has created the word solitude to express the glory of being alone.
>
> *Paul Tillich*

So let us all discover the joy and the glory of solitude.

# 21   The Positive Approach

Everything in life can be regarded either positively or negatively. Take, for example, a short walk along the street. We see uneven pavement, shabby paint on a front gate, the grass verge muddy and fouled by dogs, broken cans in the gutter, a shop window crammed with dreary merchandise; and we return home depressed and weary. Yet on exactly the same stretch of road may be seen a buddleia in full bloom sprouting from a crevice in an old wall, a robin darting along a branch, bright window boxes, a colourful display of fruit stacked outside the greengrocer's, and the gleam of blue sky reflected in a rain puddle. Having been uplifted by the sight of these, we are cheerful and relaxed on our return. We have travelled along the same road; everything mentioned was there, but we chose those on which we would focus our attention.

When I took my elderly aunt out in her wheelchair, I found it very difficult to manage if we were on a road with no pavements. Most roads are built with a camber, arching slightly at the centre, so that rain water is deflected into the gutter. This meant that the wheels of the chair would constantly turn to the side of the road, and we would proceed in a curious crab-like manner. After a while, though, I discovered that by pulling against the slope of the road, I could continue in a straight line. This became progressively easier, as I learnt to control the wheels and exert the correct pressure.

In a similar way, we have to discover how to counteract

the negative pull and deliberately turn towards the positive. When we are lonely or depressed that downward drag is very strong, and we seem inevitably drawn in that direction. We look on the black side of life, every small task becomes a formidable problem, we anticipate trouble and expect the worst. We need to struggle to reverse this frame of mind by forcing ourselves all the time to concentrate on the good, cheerful and hopeful side of life, until our thoughts begin to turn naturally in that direction.

The word 'but' is a useful one. We can use it in this way:-

It's raining today, BUT it will refresh the garden, cleanse the streets, clear the air, prevent a drought etc.

I'm exhausted, BUT I did manage to do all the shopping, clean the house, walk home and save the bus fare etc.

I didn't succeed, BUT I can try again, I've learnt from the experience, I can improve on my first attempt etc.

We will find that, despite adversity, we can still go on; we can believe in the sun, even when it is not shining.

It is fortunate indeed for us that life is divided into small compartments; that we can take one day at a time. We start completely afresh every morning. The slate is washed clean and the failures of yesterday set aside as we embark upon today. How much better, then, not to greet the dawn with a negative, "Oh God, it's morning!" but rather, positively, "Good morning, God!"

## Clouds

Look for the silver lining
Whenever there are clouds in the sky.
Remember, somewhere the sun is shining,
And so the right thing to do
Is make the sun come through.
A heart filled with joy and gladness
Will always banish sorrow and strife –
So, always look for the silver lining
And try to find the sunny side of life.

Many of you will know the words of this old song, a popular one when I was young. When we are sad and lonely there appears to be a complete absence of sunshine. It is helpful to bear two things in mind. First, that both sunshine and rain are necessary for life: all sun makes a desert; all rain a flood. Secondly, that the sun is stronger than the rain clouds which it has, in fact, created. Without sunshine there would be no clouds, for the sun sucks up water, forming it into clouds of vapour which will later fall as rain. I have seen a film of storm clouds forming over a desert, but before they are thick enough to bring rain they are burnt up by the sun as its heat intensifies throughout the day. If we can think of our sadness merely as temporary cloud which will inevitably pass, it becomes easier to bear.

The problems of pain and suffering and evil have been with mankind since the beginning of time and it is not easy to understand why they should exist, if we believe that the world has a purpose and was created by a God of love and goodness. But it seems to me that all things must have a reverse side; that good could not exist without its opposite of evil, and that before we can be caring and sympathetic towards others, we ourselves must have experienced sorrow and loss. Once the evil and negative side of life is known and understood, we are able to turn towards the good and positive. Perhaps this is the whole reason for our living.

Have you ever seen the dazzling effect of sunshine on storm clouds when that bright lining transformation is achieved? The wonderful colours of sunset would not be there if it was not for the presence of clouds. In a recent holiday in the Lake District I noticed how much more beautiful the fells and lakes appeared when there were clouds in the sky. The combination of sunlight and shadow was remarkable, and the constantly changing scene held me spellbound.

There are many dark and unpleasant experiences in life,

but equally there are unexpected times of joy and gladness which very often follow a period of suffering. Few of us have to cope with a life of unmitigated gloom, just as no one can expect to escape unscathed from pain or bereavement during a lifetime. Clouds always pass. We have to set ourselves to climb through them, step by step, until we reach again the sun that shines above them. It is then, when we emerge, that the 'silver lining' will appear, and we will know that we are stronger and have overcome yet another of life's problems.

## I can't or I can

"They can conquer who believe they can", says the old proverb. It is true. The first step happens in the mind. We are lonely or depressed and want to give up. We have to assert our will, and determine to go on.

In the old Greek legend, Hercules was given twelve tasks to do that seemed utterly beyond human strength. They were designed to kill him, and no one thought he had any chance of succeeding. But he did. His victory was achieved by refusing to admit that they WERE impossible. He knew he was strong enough to overcome them, and he tackled them steadily and patiently, one by one, until he had worked his way through them all to his final triumph.

If we feel that we must give up, because we have so much to do that we do not know where to begin, it helps to just keep plodding on, without considering the possibility of failure. When my mother was ill, one of the district nurses would constantly complain about the amount of work she had to get through in a day, and that she did not know how she could cope with it. She would spend a long while telling us about all she still had to do, and I used to think that if she were to get on with attending to my mother, she would then have more time at her disposal for her other cases. Playing some favourite music on the tape recorder will often help to get us through tedious household chores. "Music While You Work" was introduced during the war years when many people were doing dull factory work, and boredom was slowing them down. It was proved that production went up to a marked degree when employees were working to cheerful, lively music.

I have a friend with multiple sclerosis. She has no use at all in her muscles, and has to be fed and to remain in bed all day. Some years ago she was given a 'Possum' machine. The word 'possum' means in Latin 'I can', or 'I am able'. With that machine, which she operates with her mouth by blowing down a tube, she can work a typewriter. She has written several articles for magazines, and is now working on a full-length novel.

We really can do so much more than we suppose. So, when we feel, 'I can't', we must change that thought to, 'Yes, I can!' We must make 'possum' our motto. In the words of the old song, "Pick yourself up, dust yourself down, and start all over again".

## Faith

Those who have a religious faith are never completely alone. They may be lonely, but it is not the utter desolation of feeling completely isolated in the universe. To believe in God, is to accept that He has a place and purpose for us; that there is meaning in our lives, even when to us the future appears to be barren and empty. To be able to pray, means that we do not have to shut inside ourselves those feelings of futility, grief and desolation. We can reach out and find comfort, strength and guidance. For there are times in life when periods of loneliness cannot be cured, but only endured. We may be popular, out-going and carefree, surrounded by friends and supported by a caring family, but all of us in times of bereavement, serious illness or misfortune, and, of course, at our own death, must for a while walk alone. It is then that faith supports us and eases the grief or fear.

These words from the Old Testament, "I will not leave thee, nor forsake thee", and these from the New, "Lo, I am with you always", have been a comfort and inspiration to many in times of loneliness.

Two prayers for the lonely:-

> I live alone, dear lord,
> Stay by my side.
> In all my daily needs
> Be Thou my guide.
> Grant me good health,
> For that indeed I pray
> To carry on my work
> From day to day.
> Keep pure my mind
> My thoughts, my every deed.
> Let me be kind, unselfish
> In my neighbour's need.
> Save me from fire, from flood,
> Malicious tongues,
> From thieves, from fear,
> And from evil ones.
> If sickness or an accident befall
> Then, humbly, Lord, I pray
> Hear Thou my call.
> And when I'm feeling low,
> Or in despair
> Lift up my heart
> And help me in my prayer.
> I live alone, dear Lord,
> Yet have no fear,
> Because I feel your presence
> Ever near.

> O God of love, who art in all places and times, pour the balm of thy comfort upon every lonely heart.

Have pity upon those who are bereft of human love, and on those to whom it has never come. Be unto them a strong consolation, and in the end give them fulness of joy.

Amen        Anon. 1888

# Positive and Negative Actions

## To Live Alone Successfully

DO      make your home comfortable and pleasing to you.

DO      ensure that it is safe and secure.

DO      provide adequate warmth.

DO      eat a sensible diet.

DO      keep fully occupied.

DON'T  economise at the expense of your health and safety.

DON'T  keep large sums of money in the house.

DON'T  leave the door key where it can easily be found.

DON'T  admit strangers without first checking their identity.

## To Find Friends

DO      seek others needing friendship.

DO      respect confidences.

DO      listen rather than talk. Shy people are good at this.

DO      look for those who share your interests.

DO      learn to enjoy your own company. You will not then feel resentment at being alone.

DON'T  expect gratitude. It is never given in exchange in carefully weighed parcels.

DON'T   pass on gossip. Say only good things; keep other information to yourself.

DON'T   be over-critical.

DON'T   try to buy friendship. This only causes embarassment.

DON'T   constantly grumble when you talk to others.

DON'T   force a friendship. Let it grow naturally.

# Recommended Books

*Depression – The Way out of Your Prison.* Dr. Dorothy Rowe. Routledge, 1983.

*Self Help for Your Nerves.* Dr. Claire Weekes. Angus & Robertson, 1962.

*Peace from Nervous Suffering.* Dr. Claire Weekes. Angus & Robertson.

*A Handbook for Retirement – The Time of Your Life.* Published by Help The Aged, 1979.

*Alone Again – How to Cope with Bereavement and Separation.* Angela Williams. National Marriage Guidance Council, 1977.

*Staying Put – Help for Older Home Owners.* Published by Age Concern.

*Thoughts on Life to Come.* (This is a very comforting little book for the bereaved) Obtainable from Mrs M Oakley, 24 Lawrence Grove, Henleaze, Bristol BS9 4EJ 55p including postage, 1984.

*Which Way to Buy, Sell and Move House.* The Consumers' Association publishers of "WHICH?"

*The Allergy Relief Programme.* Alan Scot Levin MD and Merla Zellerbach. Gateway Books, 1983.

# Cassettes

For relaxation techniques – Mrs D Darby, 174 Surrenden Road, Brighton, Sussex BN1 6NN.

For various phobias – Lifeskills Cassettes, 3 Brighton Road, London N2.

*Relaxation for Everyday Living.* Mary Barfield, 2 Toot Rock Coastguards, Pett Level, East Sussex TN35 4EW.

# Helpful Addresses

AGE CONCERN (England), Bernard Sunley House, 60 Pitcairn Road, Mitcham, Surrey CR4 3LL. (Scotland), 33 Castle Street, Edinburgh EH2 3DN.

ASSOCIATION FOR POST NATAL ILLNESS. 7 Gowan Avenue, Fulham, London SW6.

CONTACT (for isolated elderly people), 15 Henrietta Street, Covent Garden, London WC2E 8QH.

CRUSE, CRUSE House, 126 Sheen Rd., Richmond, Surrey TW9 1VR.

DEPRESSIVES ANONYMOUS, 36 Chestnut Avenue, Beverley, N Humberside HU17 9QU.

DEPRESSIVES ASSOCIATED, P.O. Box 5, Castle Town, Portland, Dorset DT5 1BQ.

MANIC DEPRESSION FELLOWSHIP, 51 Sheen Road, Richmond-upon-Thames, Surrey.

NATIONAL ASSOCIATION FOR THE DIVORCED AND SEPARATED, 13 High St. Little Shelford, Cambridge CB2 5ES.

NATIONAL ASSOCIATION OF WIDOWS, Stafford District Voluntary Service Centre, Chell Road, Stafford ST16 2QA.

NATIONAL FEDERATION OF SOLO CLUBS, 8 Ruskin Chambers, 191 Corporation Street, Birmingham B4 6RY.

THE NATIONAL MARRIAGE GUIDANCE COUNCIL, Herbert Gray College, Little Church St, Rugby, Warwicks CV21 3AP.

THE OPEN DOOR ASSOCIATION (for agoraphobics), 447 Pensby Road, Heswall, Wirral, Cheshire L61 9PQ.

'ONE' MAGAZINE (runs 'Mags' – circular letters for people with similar interests), 8 Dukes Close, North Weald, Epping, Essex CM16 6DA.

THE PHOBICS SOCIETY, 4 Cheltenham Road, Chorlton-cum-Hardy, Manchester M21 1QN.

PORTIA TRUST (pubs. mag. for lonely people), 15 Senhouse Street, Maryport, Cumbria CA15 6AB.

RELAXATION FOR LIVING (publish many useful leaflets), 29 Burwood Park Rd, Walton-on-Thames, Surrey KT12 5LH.

THE SAMARITANS (See phone book for local address)

WOMEN'S ROYAL VOLUNTARY SERVICE, 17 Old Park Lane, London W1Y 4AJ. (Local branches undertake voluntary work in a variety of areas – eg. helping the elderly or handicapped, running clubs etc.)